AFRICAN POLITICAL, ECONOMIC,

DEMOCRATIC REPUBLIC OF CONGO

CONDITIONS, ISSUES AND U.S. RELATIONS

AFRICAN POLITICAL, ECONOMIC, AND SECURITY ISSUES

Additional books in this series can be found on Nova's website
under the Series tab.

Additional e-books in this series can be found on Nova's website
under the e-book tab.

DEMOCRATIC REPUBLIC OF CONGO

CONDITIONS, ISSUES AND U.S. RELATIONS

SHELBY RAKE

EDITOR

New York

Library of Congress Cataloging-in-Publication Data

ISBN 978-1-63117-544-2

Published by Nova Science Publishers, Inc. † New York

CONTENTS

PREFACE

Insecurity, poor governance, and a long-running humanitarian crisis in the Democratic Republic of Congo (DRC) present a range of challenges for U.S. policymakers, including the U.S. Congress. Chronic instability in eastern DRC, an area rich in minerals and other natural resources, has caused widespread human suffering and inhibited private sector investment throughout the Great Lakes region—which includes DRC and its neighbors to the east. This book discusses the background and United States policy of the Democratic Republic of Congo, and provides insight on the DRC's conditions and issues.

Chapter 1 - Insecurity, poor governance, and a long-running humanitarian crisis in the Democratic Republic of Congo (DRC) present a range of challenges for U.S. policymakers, including the U.S. Congress. Chronic instability in eastern DRC, an area rich in minerals and other natural resources, has caused widespread human suffering and inhibited private sector investment throughout the Great Lakes region—which includes DRC and its neighbors to the east. Donors, including the United States, have recently increased their diplomatic engagement in DRC, but prospects for the future remain uncertain. Congolese political actors have often displayed limited capacity and will to improve security and government accountability, while several of DRC's neighbors have reportedly provided cyclical support to nonstate armed groups within DRC.

In recent months, DRC and its neighbors have signed a regional peace framework; the United Nations (U.N.) and the Obama Administration have appointed special envoys to the region; and the U.N. Security Council has authorized an "Intervention Brigade" within the existing U.N. peacekeeping operation in DRC (MONUSCO) to conduct operations against armed groups in the east. These developments have raised hopes of progress, although similar efforts in the past have proven unable to bring lasting peace. While the Obama Administration has recently suggested that it will devote high-level attention to DRC and the region, U.S. leverage may be constrained by available resources, limited DRC capacity and commitment, and the challenge of coordinating with and influencing other key players, including European donors, China, and regional actors such as Rwanda, Uganda, Angola, and South Africa. U.S. policymakers, including in Congress, continue to debate the relative effectiveness of various policy tools in DRC, such as aid, diplomacy, and other forms of engagement.

The United States has a long history of diplomatic, economic, and security engagements in DRC and neighboring states. It has facilitated past regional peace accords and provided billions of dollars in bilateral and multilateral aid over the past decade. Annual bilateral aid to DRC has totaled $200 million-$300 million in recent years, in addition to roughly $50 million-$150 million annually in emergency humanitarian aid and $400 million-$600 million in annual contributions to MONUSCO. Under an executive order in place since 2006, the United States has imposed targeted sanctions against persons responsible for arms trafficking and human rights violations in DRC. As a permanent member of the U.N. Security Council, the United States also shapes the authorization of MONUSCO and U.N. sanctions, and it wields influence within the international financial institutions that provide crucial funding and technical support to the DRC government.

Congress has used a range of tools to shape U.S. policy toward DRC and the region, including hearings, legislation, and oversight activities. Congress authorizes, appropriates, and oversees U.S. foreign aid funding for DRC and neighboring states. In DRC, such funding supports programs seeking to address health and humanitarian needs, advance democratic governance, encourage economic growth and development, support military professionalization, and end the regional trade in "conflict minerals," among other goals. Congress also appropriates funding in support of U.S. assessed contributions to MONUSCO's budget, to which the United States is the largest donor. Based on long-standing human rights concerns, Congress has placed legal restrictions on certain types of U.S. aid to DRC, and has conditioned the provision of certain types of military aid to Rwanda and Uganda on their noninterference in eastern DRC. Two DRC- related resolutions have been introduced during the 113th Congress: H.Res. 131 and S.Res. 144.

Chapter 2 - The Democratic Republic of the Congo (DRC) is a nominally centralized, constitutional republic. The president and the lower house of parliament (National Assembly) are popularly elected. Provincial assemblies choose the members of the upper house (Senate). In November 2011 the country held multiparty presidential and National Assembly elections, which many local and international observers judged lacked credibility and were seriously flawed. There were many instances in which state security forces (SSF) acted independently of civilian control and of military command.

Weak civilian control over SSF contributed to increased conflict in eastern Congo. In April integrated former rebels of the National Congress for the Defense of the People (CNDP) defected from the national army (FARDC). Subsequently, they created the M23 armed group (named after the March 23, 2009, peace agreements) and challenged government control in the eastern part of the country, which led to violence, the displacement of large numbers of persons, and significant human rights abuses, including the M23's recruitment and use of children in armed conflict. During the year the government entered into a UN-backed action plan to end the recruitment and use of child soldiers, and the government made significant improvements to reduce the presence of children in the nation's armed forces.

The three most important human rights issues were: armed conflict in the East that exacerbated an already precarious human rights situation, particularly with regard to sexual- and gender-based violence (SGBV); the lack of an independent and effective judiciary; and impunity throughout the country for many serious abuses, including unlawful killings, disappearances, torture, rape, and arbitrary arrests and detention.

Other major human rights problems included the following: severe and life- threatening conditions in prison and detention facilities; prolonged pretrial detention; arbitrary interference with privacy, family, and home; SSF members abusing, threatening, and obstructing journalists, human rights advocates, and the work of UN investigators; abuse of internally displaced persons (IDPs) by SSF and rebel and militia groups (RMG); widespread official corruption; SSF and RMG retention and recruitment of child soldiers; and use of forced civilian labor. Societal discrimination and abuse, particularly against women, children, persons with disabilities, as well as lesbian, gay, bisexual, and transgender (LGBT) persons, and persons with albinism; enslavement of Pygmies; trafficking in persons; child labor; and lack of protection of workers' rights were also problems.

Despite some modest improvements, impunity for human rights abuses remained a severe problem in the security services. Authorities did not prosecute or punish the great majority of abusers.

RMG, some of which were supported by foreign governments and militaries, committed violent abuses against civilians, particularly in North Kivu, South Kivu, and Orientale provinces. The abuses--some of which may constitute war crimes-- included unlawful killings, disappearances, torture, and SGBV. RMG also recruited, abducted, and retained child soldiers and compelled forced labor. RMG and some army units engaged in the illegal exploitation and trade of natural resources in the East. In a separate conflict in the Haut Uele and Bas Uele districts of Orientale Province, the Lord's Resistance Army (LRA) continued to commit serious human rights violations through attacks resulting in deaths, injuries, abductions, forced labor, looting, and general insecurity.

Chapter 3 - The constitution and other laws and policies protect religious freedom and, in practice, the government generally respected religious freedom. The trend in the government's respect for religious freedom did not change significantly during the year.

There were no reports of societal abuses or discrimination based on religious affiliation, belief, or practice.

U.S. embassy representatives discussed religious freedom with the government and routinely met with religious leaders of all faiths.

Chapter 4 - 2013 Investment Climate Statement: Democratic Republic of Congo by Bureau of Economic and Business Affairs.

In: Democratic Republic of Congo
Editor: Shelby Rake

ISBN: 978-1-63117-544-2
© 2014 Nova Science Publishers, Inc.

Chapter 1

DEMOCRATIC REPUBLIC OF CONGO: BACKGROUND AND U.S. POLICY*

Alexis Arieff and Thomas Coen

SUMMARY

Insecurity, poor governance, and a long-running humanitarian crisis in the Democratic Republic of Congo (DRC) present a range of challenges for U.S. policymakers, including the U.S. Congress. Chronic instability in eastern DRC, an area rich in minerals and other natural resources, has caused widespread human suffering and inhibited private sector investment throughout the Great Lakes region—which includes DRC and its neighbors to the east. Donors, including the United States, have recently increased their diplomatic engagement in DRC, but prospects for the future remain uncertain. Congolese political actors have often displayed limited capacity and will to improve security and government accountability, while several of DRC's neighbors have reportedly provided cyclical support to nonstate armed groups within DRC.

In recent months, DRC and its neighbors have signed a regional peace framework; the United Nations (U.N.) and the Obama Administration have appointed special envoys to the region; and the U.N. Security Council has

---

* This is an edited, reformatted and augmented version of a Congressional Research Service publication, CRS Report for Congress, R43166, dated July 29, 2013.

authorized an "Intervention Brigade" within the existing U.N. peacekeeping operation in DRC (MONUSCO) to conduct operations against armed groups in the east. These developments have raised hopes of progress, although similar efforts in the past have proven unable to bring lasting peace. While the Obama Administration has recently suggested that it will devote high-level attention to DRC and the region, U.S. leverage may be constrained by available resources, limited DRC capacity and commitment, and the challenge of coordinating with and influencing other key players, including European donors, China, and regional actors such as Rwanda, Uganda, Angola, and South Africa. U.S. policymakers, including in Congress, continue to debate the relative effectiveness of various policy tools in DRC, such as aid, diplomacy, and other forms of engagement.

The United States has a long history of diplomatic, economic, and security engagements in DRC and neighboring states. It has facilitated past regional peace accords and provided billions of dollars in bilateral and multilateral aid over the past decade. Annual bilateral aid to DRC has totaled $200 million-$300 million in recent years, in addition to roughly $50 million-$150 million annually in emergency humanitarian aid and $400 million-$600 million in annual contributions to MONUSCO. Under an executive order in place since 2006, the United States has imposed targeted sanctions against persons responsible for arms trafficking and human rights violations in DRC. As a permanent member of the U.N. Security Council, the United States also shapes the authorization of MONUSCO and U.N. sanctions, and it wields influence within the international financial institutions that provide crucial funding and technical support to the DRC government.

Congress has used a range of tools to shape U.S. policy toward DRC and the region, including hearings, legislation, and oversight activities. Congress authorizes, appropriates, and oversees U.S. foreign aid funding for DRC and neighboring states. In DRC, such funding supports programs seeking to address health and humanitarian needs, advance democratic governance, encourage economic growth and development, support military professionalization, and end the regional trade in "conflict minerals," among other goals. Congress also appropriates funding in support of U.S. assessed contributions to MONUSCO's budget, to which the United States is the largest donor. Based on long-standing human rights concerns, Congress has placed legal restrictions on certain types of U.S. aid to DRC, and has conditioned the provision of certain types of military aid to Rwanda and Uganda on their noninterference in eastern DRC. Two DRC- related resolutions have been introduced during the 113th Congress: H.Res. 131 and S.Res. 144.

OVERVIEW

The Democratic Republic of Congo (DRC) emerged from seven years of civil and regional war in 2003, but continues to face stark challenges. Despite international partners' hopes for increased democratization and reforms following landmark 2006 elections—the first relatively free and fair vote since independence from Belgium in 1960—the state remains weak and dysfunctional. State actors often appear more focused on controlling resources and personal power than on establishing security, creating effective state institutions, and fostering socioeconomic development for the country's 75 million inhabitants.

In contrast to 2006, international observers characterized the 2011 elections that returned President Joseph Kabila to office as deeply flawed, underscoring the fragility of the government's legitimacy. Since early 2012, President Kabila has also struggled to quell a new rebellion in the restive eastern province of North Kivu, by a group known as the M23. Recurrent conflict in the mineral-rich, agriculturally fertile, and densely inhabited east stems from deep tensions related to resources, land, ethnicity, citizenship, military reform, and regional geopolitics, as well as criminal motivations. It also reflects a complex pattern of state negligence, incapacity, and coercion throughout the country, most of which is not directly affected by conflict.

Economic growth, buoyed by high global commodity prices, has been relatively strong in recent years (7% in 2012). DRC also receives high levels of outside aid, with over $5.5 billion in net official development assistance in 2011—equivalent to 35.3% of GDP.[1] Yet despite vast mineral riches, water resources, and agricultural potential, the majority of Congolese live in poverty, and food insecurity is widespread.[2] About 2.6 million Congolese are internally displaced, and nearly a half-million more have fled to nearby countries as refugees.[3] The U.N. consolidated appeal for humanitarian aid for DRC is the fifth largest in the world.[4] DRC is tied for last place on the U.N. Human Development Index and has the world's lowest per-capita gross domestic product (GDP). As the 11th-largest country in the world by area, DRC exhibits great internal diversity; some areas, such as the mineral-rich Katanga province, have enjoyed comparative stability and prosperity. However, recent militia violence suggests that even this relative security is tenuous.[5]

The United Nations (U.N.) Organization Stabilization Operation in DRC (known as MONUSCO, its French acronym), with some 17,000 military personnel, provides support for security and the extension of state authority in the east, with limited success according to many observers.[6]

Population Displacements (Multiple Causes) and Approximate M23-Controlled Area

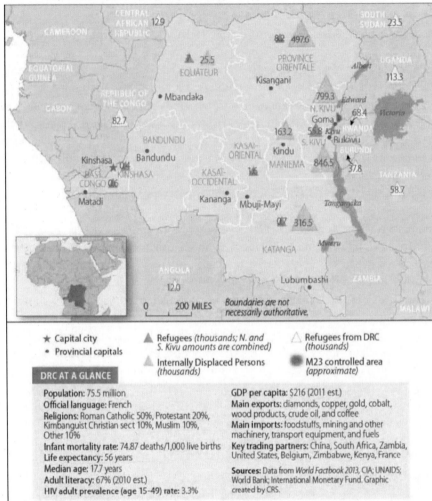

Source: CRS, based on reports by U.S. and U.N. agencies, news agencies, and nongovernmental organizations. Base map created by Hannah Fischer using Esri basemaps and world cities.

Note: Refugee and internal displacement figures date from late 2012-early 2013, and shift regularly.

Figure 1. Map of the Democratic Republic of Congo.

In February 2013, the U.N. facilitated a regional "Framework Agreement" (discussed below) that aims to define the responsibilities of the DRC government, regional states, and donors in ending the cyclical conflict in DRC. A newly appointed U.N. Special Envoy of the Secretary-General, Mary Robinson, former president of Ireland and U.N. High Commissioner for Human Rights (1997-2002), is expected to lead international efforts to enforce the agreement and develop benchmarks for implementation. In March 2013, the U.N. Security Council authorized a new "Intervention Brigade" within MONUSCO, tasked with "neutralizing" nonstate armed groups in the east, including the M23. Whether the agreement and new component of MONUSCO have the potential to break the cycle of regional instability and humanitarian suffering remains to be seen.

The United States has a long history of diplomatic, economic, and security engagements in DRC and the region. U.S. policy is focused on regional stability, DRC's economic importance as a source of global mineral commodities, its democracy and governance trajectory, and efforts to address human rights abuses—particularly violence against women—and to curtail the trade in "conflict minerals."[7] U.S. assistance to Uganda's military also supports efforts to counter the Lord's Resistance Army (LRA) in DRC and neighboring states.[8] The Obama Administration recently elevated its diplomatic engagement by appointing former Senator Russ Feingold as U.S. Special Envoy to the Great Lakes region. In making the announcement, Secretary of State John Kerry said that achieving a lasting peace in Congo is a "high-level priority" with "very significant" stakes.[9] U.S. policymakers continue to assess the implications of DRC's flawed 2011 elections and renewed conflict in the east—which point to the potential limitations of donor-supported stabilization and democracy-promotion efforts—for U.S. policy and aid programs.

Congressional Actions

Congress has shaped U.S. policy toward DRC and the Great Lakes region, including through its authorization, appropriation, and oversight of U.S. foreign assistance. Additional details on relevant public laws can be found in the **Appendix**. Recent congressional actions include:

- Holding regular hearings on the situation in DRC and U.S. policy responses;

- Seeking to define U.S. policy toward DRC and authorizing certain policy and foreign aid responses to the conflict in the east (e.g., P.L. 109-456);
- Appropriating foreign assistance funds for specific purposes in DRC, particularly related to military professionalization and the prevention and treatment of sexual and gender-based violence (e.g., P.L. 111-32, P.L. 111-212);
- Restricting certain types of bilateral aid to DRC based on human rights concerns, particularly related to the DRC military's reported use of child soldiers (e.g., P.L. 110-457, P.L. 112-10, P.L. 112-74) and the country's reported failure to meet minimal standards in responding to human trafficking (P.L. 106-386, as amended)[10];
- Restricting certain military aid to Rwanda and Uganda if they are found to support rebel groups in eastern DRC (P.L. 112-74);
- Requiring the executive branch to formulate a strategy to guide U.S. efforts to eliminate the regional threat of the Lord's Resistance Army (P.L. 111-172);
- Requiring the Securities and Exchange Commission (SEC) to regulate international trade in Central African "conflict minerals," that is, ores of tantalum and niobium, tin, tungsten, and gold, and their derivatives (P.L. 111-203); and
- Authorizing targeted sanctions against persons found to be providing support to the M23, a rebel group formed in 2012 (P.L. 112-239).

Two resolutions on U.S. policy toward DRC have been introduced in the 113th Congress: H.Res. 131 and S.Res. 144. The latter was agreed to in the Senate on June 26, 2013. Broadly, these resolutions call on regional and international actors to contribute to greater security and stability, and on the Obama Administration to provide multi-faceted support for regional peace.

Background

With its resources, vast territory, and strategic position, DRC has long served as an arena of regional and international competition. "Congo Free State" was claimed in 1885 as the personal possession of Belgian King Leopold II. King Leopold's administration became notorious for its plundering of Congo's natural resources and its human rights abuses, leading the Belgian government to transition the territory into a formal colony in 1908.[11]

In 1960, Congo gained independence, after parliamentary elections that led nationalist leader Patrice Lumumba to become prime minister. The country's early years were plagued by instability, including an armed secession movement in Katanga and an army mutiny that culminated in Lumumba's murder in early 1961.[12] One of the first U.N. peacekeeping operations deployed in response to the Katanga crisis in 1960 and stayed until 1964.

In 1965, Colonel Joseph Mobutu, who had been involved in the mutiny against Lumumba, seized power in a coup, gradually instituting a more centralized and authoritarian form of government. Mobutu's claims to promote a more "authentic," indigenous Congolese national identity led him to rename himself Mobutu Sese Seko and the country Zaire. Mobutu's 32-year rule drew on U.S. and other Western support in the context of Cold War rivalry over the loyalty of African leaders.[13] He also employed tools such as fraudulent elections, brute force, and patronage networks fueled by extensive official corruption, leading many analysts to view his regime as a "kleptocracy."[14] At the same time, petty corruption provided a crucial economic safety net for many Congolese.

Domestic and international pressures on Mobutu mounted as the Cold War drew to a close, and as the aging president's health faltered. Mobutu agreed in principle to a multi-party democratic system in 1990, but elections were repeatedly delayed. State institutions and the military progressively deteriorated, while regional civil conflicts and the genocide in neighboring Rwanda spilled over the border, diverting state resources and destabilizing local communities. In the aftermath of the 1994 Rwandan genocide, ethnic Hutu extremist forces fleeing the new Tutsi-dominated government in Rwanda used refugee camps in Zaire as bases to attack Rwanda, with reported backing from Mobutu. Partly in response, Rwanda and Uganda backed a rebellion against Mobutu led by an exiled Congolese militant, Laurent Désiré Kabila. This later became known as the "first" Congo war. With Mobutu's security forces and personal health in tatters, the rebellion succeeded, and Kabila became president in 1997, renaming the country DRC.

Tensions between the erstwhile allies soon erupted. In 1998, amid growing public hostility toward Congolese Tutsis and the presence of Rwandan soldiers in DRC, the government announced that Rwandan troops would be expelled. In response, Tutsi soldiers rebelled. Rwanda and Uganda then intervened again, deploying troops into DRC and cultivating local rebel proxies, this time in an effort to unseat Kabila. Angola, Zimbabwe, Sudan, and others joined the fight on Kabila's side. The conflict, dubbed "Africa's World War," led to a major humanitarian crisis.[15]

RWANDA'S REPORTED INVOLVEMENT IN DRC CONFLICTS

According to numerous independent reports, Rwanda has periodically intervened in the recurring conflict in eastern DRC, and has cultivated a series of Congolese armed and political proxy groups in DRC since the mid-1990s.[16] U.S. officials have recently publicly referenced reported Rwandan support for the M23 rebel group (see "U.S. Policy"). These alleged interventions by Rwanda might have been motivated by factors related to its own national security considerations; the two countries' intertwined histories and populations; and economic incentives. While strongly refuting allegations of involvement in DRC conflicts, Rwandan officials often contend that the DRC has failed to rein in—and indeed has, at times, collaborated with—armed groups operating on Congolese soil that pose a security threat to Rwanda. These notably include the Democratic Forces for the Liberation of Rwanda or FDLR, which was founded by ethnic Hutu extremists involved in the 1994 Rwandan genocide.[17] Rwandans also point to Congolese efforts to deny land, citizenship, and other rights to ethnic communities of Rwandan origin in the Kivus, and to periodic violence targeting these communities. Some observers contend that alleged Rwandan intervention in DRC has also been motivated by involvement in resource smuggling.[18]

In 2001, President Laurent Kabila was assassinated by one of his bodyguards. His son Joseph Kabila assumed the presidency and continued a process of peace talks. A 2002 peace accord called for the withdrawal of foreign troops and the integration of rebel groups into the military and government. A transitional government was put in place from 2003 until national elections in 2006, which were largely funded and managed by international donors and the U.N. peacekeeping operation. President Kabila was returned to office in that election, following a tense and violent run-off against former rebel leader Jean-Pierre Bemba. He was re-elected in 2011 (see "Democracy and Governance Challenges").

Congolese relations with Uganda, Rwanda, and Angola remain complex and volatile, although the latter is sometimes viewed as a Kabila ally.

Relations with Rwanda have been periodically inflamed by reports that Rwanda has, at times, backed insurgent groups in eastern DRC (see **text box** above). In 2008, Kabila and Rwandan President Paul Kagame reached a fragile rapprochement, leading to the reestablishment of bilateral diplomatic ties in 2009. However, this and several efforts to integrate rebel groups into state institutions did not end the cycle of conflict.

SELECTED ISSUES

Democracy and Governance Challenges

Presidential and parliamentary elections held in November 2011, the first ever to be organized and financed primarily by the Congolese government, were widely perceived as a test of DRC's fragile post-conflict transition. International observers had viewed the 2006 elections as basically credible, despite procedural shortcomings and significant election-related violence.[19] However, after an electoral period characterized by delays, disputes over the independence of key electoral institutions, and instances of violence, Western and domestic election observers concluded that the 2011 electoral process lacked credibility.[20] The vote also took place in an uneven playing field between incumbent President Kabila and his 10 rival candidates, with Kabila enjoying significant media, financial, and resource advantages and employing state security forces to harass the opposition. The National Assembly had also recently amended the constitution to allow the presidential candidate with the most votes to win short of a majority, without requiring a run-off.

President Kabila was declared the winner of the presidential election with 49% of the vote. His closest rival, veteran opposition leader Etienne Tshisekedi, received 32%, according to the official tally. Tshisekedi rejected the results, declared himself president, and called—mostly unsuccessfully— for protests and for members of his Union For Democracy and Social Progress (UDPS) party who were elected to parliament not to take up their seats. Kabila's People's Party for Reconstruction and Democracy (PPRD) lost seats in the legislature in 2011 compared to 2006, but nevertheless assembled a majority coalition. As with the presidential election, the U.S.-funded Carter Center criticized "the integrity of the national assembly results," faulting in particular the National Independent Election Committee's (CENI's) handling of vote tabulation. Some observers viewed the CENI as biased in favor of

Kabila.[21] Since the elections, Kabila has made limited overtures to political opponents, and the government has, at times, deployed security forces to harass opposition figures, including Tshisekedi.

Substantial power is concentrated in the presidency, but some local and provincial officials—such as the governor of Katanga, Moïse Katumbi Chapwe—appear to wield significant authority locally. Provincial and local elections, expected to be held soon after the 2011 polls, were instead repeatedly delayed as Kabila focused on solidifying his control, and as available funding appeared limited. As senators are elected by provincial assemblies, senatorial elections were therefore indirectly delayed; there have never been post-conflict local elections. The electoral timetable may be tied to broader efforts toward decentralization, including nominal plans for national redistricting. These plans are likely to confront significant resistance among powerful figures who benefit from the current electoral and governance structure. Some analysts have also recently raised concerns that the constitution could be amended again to allow Kabila to run for another term in 2016.[22]

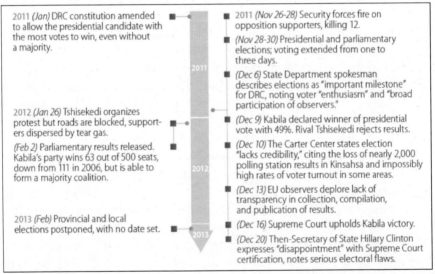

Source: CRS, based on reports by U.S. and U.N. agencies, news agencies, and nongovernmental organizations.

Figure 2. DRC's 2011 Elections:Timeline.

Beyond the electoral process, the DRC has immense governance problems. Transparency International's 2012 Corruptions Perceptions Index ranks the DRC 160 out of 174 countries. The state's ability to manage and monitor extraction of its natural resources has been a perennial and crucial challenge (see "The Mining Sector"). Public service delivery is hampered by the fact that outside of Kinshasa, the central government has only nominal control over large swaths of its land and must contend with poor transportation and electricity infrastructure, challenging terrain, and protracted local conflicts. A decrepit agriculture sector and continued conflict have contributed to severe food insecurity, despite abundant fertile land and water resources.[23]

Conflict in the Kivus

Conflict and insecurity are particularly acute in the densely inhabited and mineral-rich North and South Kivu provinces in the east, an epicenter of regional unrest since the 1990s. The spillover of conflicts in Rwanda and Burundi in the 1990s aggravated long-standing tensions in the region between and among communities self-identified as "indigenous" and those that trace their ethnic origins (however distant) to Rwanda. These dynamics have been entrenched by localized disputes and by regional geopolitical calculations. The Armed Forces of DRC (known as the FARDC after its French acronym) and other state security forces have been implicated in human rights atrocities in the east, such as looting, killings, and mass rapes, including during operations against abusive nonstate actors and as part of illicit involvement in the mining sector.[24]

The M23 rebellion in North Kivu is the latest iteration of cyclical conflict in the east. The M23 emerged in early 2012 after a mutiny by former members of the National Congress for the Republic of the People (CNDP), a rebel group that had been integrated into the FARDC in 2009 and thereby nominally dissolved.[25] M23 leaders claim that the DRC government did not uphold a March 23, 2009, peace accord, particularly regarding salaries and rank for ex-CNDP soldiers; the return of Congolese refugees from Rwanda; administrative reforms; and local development and reconciliation initiatives. The group has also occasionally espoused national-level aims. Some M23 commanders, several of whom are on U.S. and U.N. sanctions lists, appear motivated by self-preservation and a desire to control resource and smuggling revenues, but others are arguably driven by what they see as unequal treatment and broken promises by the government.

Available information also suggests that the M23 may have acted as a proxy or buffer force for Rwanda, which is alleged to have aided the group. Reports by U.N. Security Council sanctions monitors known as the Group of Experts (GOE) indicate that extensive and crucial material, logistical, and political support for the M23 has come from Rwanda, including via the deployment of Rwandan troops on Congolese soil. In 2012, the GOE also pointed to more "subtle" military and political support from Ugandan officials and military officers.[26] These allegations present complications for U.S. policymakers, as Rwanda and Uganda are considered key U.S. regional partners due to their leadership in U.S.-backed peacekeeping and stabilization efforts elsewhere on the continent. U.S. officials have confirmed and criticized Rwanda's reported actions (see "U.S. Policy") and called for all external support to cease. A recent GOE draft report reportedly finds more limited Rwandan support, and no Ugandan support, for the M23.[27]

In November 2012, the M23 sparked a regional crisis when it captured the key city of Goma, in fighting marked by significant human rights abuses on both sides. Talks hosted by Uganda led to the M23's withdrawal from the town within two weeks, and a subsequent U.N.-backed process culminated in the regional "Framework" accord. Eleven African countries are signatories to the agreement, including DRC, all of its neighbors (Angola, Burundi, Central African Republic, the Republic of Congo, Rwanda, South Sudan, Uganda, Tanzania, and Zambia), and South Africa.[28] Regional leaders thereby committed not to interfere in the internal affairs of neighboring states or provide support to nonstate armed groups, while DRC leaders committed to security sector and institutional reforms, the extension of state authority in the east, political decentralization, and national reconciliation. The signatories also agreed to pursue regional economic integration. If these processes, and the new U.N. "Intervention Brigade," do not lead to a political settlement and/or disarmament of remaining M23 forces, the degree to which the M23 continues to pose a threat may well hinge on its ability to expand its base beyond a narrow sub-set of North Kivu's minority Tutsi community. The group's trajectory may also depend on the calculations of neighboring states that have reportedly provided support either to the M23 or to the government.

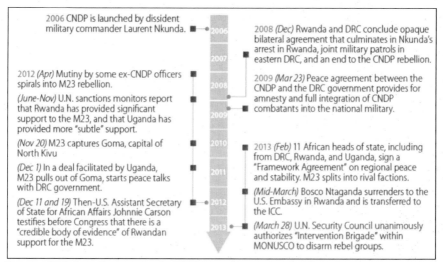

2006 CNDP is launched by dissident military commander Laurent Nkunda.

2008 *(Dec)* Rwanda and DRC conclude opaque bilateral agreement that culminates in Nkunda's arrest in Rwanda, joint military patrols in eastern DRC, and an end to the CNDP rebellion.

2012 *(Apr)* Mutiny by some ex-CNDP officers spirals into M23 rebellion.

(June-Nov) U.N. sanctions monitors report that Rwanda has provided significant support to the M23, and that Uganda has provided more "subtle" support.

2009 *(Mar 23)* Peace agreement between the CNDP and the DRC government provides for amnesty and full integration of CNDP combatants into the national military.

(Nov 20) M23 captures Goma, capital of North Kivu

(Dec 1) In a deal facilitated by Uganda, M23 pulls out of Goma, starts peace talks with DRC government.

(Dec 11 and 19) Then-U.S. Assistant Secretary of State for African Affairs Johnnie Carson testifies before Congress that there is a "credible body of evidence" of Rwandan support for the M23.

2013 *(Feb)* 11 African heads of state, including from DRC, Rwanda, and Uganda, sign a "Framework Agreement" on regional peace and stability. M23 splits into rival factions.

(Mid-March) Bosco Ntaganda surrenders to the U.S. Embassy in Rwanda and is transferred to the ICC.

(March 28) U.N. Security Council unanimously authorizes "Intervention Brigade" within MONUSCO to disarm rebel groups.

Source: CRS, based on reports by U.N. agencies, news agencies, and nongovernmental organizations.

Figure 3. The M23 Conflict: Timeline.

Other armed groups that continue to attack local populations and illicitly extract natural resources in the Kivus include the Democratic Forces for the Liberation of Rwanda (FDLR), a brutally abusive group founded by ethnic Hutu extremists who fled to Congo from Rwanda after helping to carry out the 1994 genocide there; "Mai Mai," a term that broadly refers to a disparate array of local militias; and a range of other armed groups. Elements of a Burundian Hutu-led former rebel group, the National Liberation Forces (FNL), are present, as is an obscure armed group of Ugandan origin, the Allied Democratic Forces/National Army for the Liberation of Uganda (ADF/NALU), which has carried out sporadic attacks. The Ugandan government and some analysts claim the ADF/NALU has ties to regional Islamist extremist groups.[29]

U.N. Peacekeeping Operations

In 1999, the U.N. Security Council established the U.N. Organization Mission in the Congo (MONUC) to monitor a ceasefire in DRC's civil-regional war. MONUC's mandate was gradually expanded to include a range of tasks, notably helping to organize the 2006 elections, monitoring a U.N. arms embargo and related sanctions, and supporting the Congolese military in operations against armed groups in the east. In 2010, the Security Council ended MONUC's mandate and established the U.N. Organization Stabilization Operation in Congo (MONUSCO) to replace it, emphasizing a "stabilization" rather than a "peacekeeping" role, reportedly partly in response to DRC government concerns about sovereignty. MONUSCO's current mandate authorizes its military component to take "all necessary measures" to protect civilians, pursue armed groups, help monitor the arms embargo, and support DRC efforts to arrest and prosecute individuals responsible for war crimes and crimes against humanity. The Security Council has also tasked U.N. civilian officials to "encourage and accelerate" progress on security sector reform, promote political dialogue, improve state management of natural resources, support the extension of state authority, and monitor human rights, among other tasks.

In its most recent one-year extension of MONUSCO's mandate, under U.N. Security Council Resolution 2098, adopted in March 2013, the U.N. Security Council authorized a new "Intervention Brigade" within MONUSCO's authorized troop ceiling of 19,815. The Brigade, expected to comprise 3,000 troops from South Africa, Malawi, and Tanzania, is tasked with "neutralizing" nonstate armed groups. While MONUSCO forces have regularly provided support to DRC-led military operations against rebel groups in the east under past mandates, the new mandate authorizes the Intervention Brigade to "carry out targeted offensive operations," including "unilaterally." Some analysts are hopeful that the Brigade will deter human rights violations by armed groups, pressure the M23 to negotiate a political solution to the conflict, and help protect civilians. Others, however, are skeptical that it will resolve the long-running crisis in the east, due to concerns about its capabilities and the limits of a purely military approach.

Humanitarian and Human Rights Conditions

As noted above, violence and other hardships have caused the displacement of over 3 million Congolese. About 6.4 million people in DRC face crisis- or emergency-level food insecurity, with North Kivu, South Kivu, Maniema, and Katanga the most affected provinces.[30] About 70% of

Congolese lack access to adequate food and one in four children are malnourished, according to the World Food Program. Congo was ranked last on the 2011 Global Hunger Index, a composite scale that includes indicators on undernourishment, underweight children, and child mortality, and its hunger situation was rated "extremely alarming."[31] The country also suffers from poor-to- nonexistent health infrastructure. A lack of healthcare, inadequate water and sanitation facilities, and DRC's equatorial climate have contributed to the spread of diseases eliminated in most parts of the world, with recent outbreaks of cholera, measles, Ebola, and yellow fever.

Human rights conditions are severe. The State Department has identified the three most important human rights issues as "armed conflict in the East that exacerbated an already precarious human rights situation, particularly with regard to sexual- and gender-based violence (SGBV); the lack of an independent and effective judiciary; and impunity throughout the country for many serious abuses, including unlawful killings, disappearances, torture, rape, and arbitrary arrests and detention."32 According to the department, other "major human rights problems" include the abuse of journalists, human rights advocates, and U.N. investigators by state security forces; "life-threatening" prison conditions; "widespread official corruption"; the use of child soldiers by state and rebel actors; forced labor; and trafficking in persons.

Particular international attention has been paid to the issue of sexual and gender-based violence in DRC. SGBV affects women throughout the country, across class, regional, and ethnic lines, but its scale and brutality in eastern DRC are extreme, with extensive reports of gang rape, rape in public, forced incest, rape with foreign objects, and urogenital mutilation.[33] Sexual assault is sometimes carried out as part of coordinated armed attacks, but it is also frequently opportunistic. The psycho-social and health consequences have been devastating. The DRC military has reportedly been the largest perpetrator of such abuses, seemingly due, in part, to its size and the repeated integration of abusive rebel groups.[34] Significant perpetrators of sexual violence also include nonstate armed groups such as the FDLR and Mai Mai militias. The prevalence of sexual violence has been attributed to the eroded status of women, weak state authority, a deeply flawed justice system, and a breakdown in community protection mechanisms. As with other abuses, sexual violence has also been linked to structural problems within the security forces. While women and girls are the primary targets, men and boys have also been victims. Despite legal reforms, donor pressure, and foreign assistance efforts, observers report that impunity is the norm for perpetrators of sexual crimes, and indeed for most grave human rights abuses.

U.N. peacekeepers have been criticized for failing to protect civilians from SGBV, for example in several instances of mass rape carried out near U.N. outposts, and during the November 2012 M23 seizure of Goma. U.N. peacekeepers have also been accused of sexual abuse and exploitation; in 2012, 25 such allegations were recorded against MONUSCO personnel.[35]

Security Sector Reform (SSR) Efforts

The roughly 150,000-person FARDC, formed at the end of the 1998-2003 war, reflects an attempt to forge a national military from disparate armed groups and elements of the abusive and dysfunctional Mobutu-era army. FARDC troops are not provided with consistent doctrine or training; they are also poorly and inconsistently paid, and are not given adequate food or supplies. These shortages may encourage looting and other abuses. The integration of additional armed groups into the FARDC has continued during the post-conflict period, and accelerated between 2009 and 2011, reportedly contributing to internal disarray.[36] The national police, judiciary, and other security institutions also suffer from limited capacity and a record of corruption and abuse.

Analysts and donors have viewed SSR as essential to a wide range of policy goals in DRC, including regional security; human rights improvements; and fiscal stability. Donors have supported a number of SSR programs since 2005, focusing on the military, police, and justice sector. These include a European Union advisory mission (EUSEC), which aims to reform the FARDC's administration of personnel and financing; MONUSCO-led police and military training; and bilateral train-and-equip programs administered by the United States (see "Foreign Assistance"), France, Belgium, South Africa, Angola, and China, among others. It is difficult to document clear signs of structural improvements in the security sector, however, and donor efforts appear to have been challenged by a lack of strategic planning and coordination; conflicting policy goals (structural reform versus the negotiated settlement of conflicts through integration); limited justice sector capacity; and limited political will and sustainability. While deep changes could potentially benefit the government by enabling it to project state authority, they could also threaten powerful interests within the government and Kabila's inner circle.

THE ECONOMY

The DRC has some of the largest endowments of natural resources in the world. Yet it has been unable to translate that natural wealth into benefits for its citizens, even as the economy continues to recover from severe decline during the late Mobutu era and the 1998-2003 conflict. Educational opportunity is lacking, the workforce is overwhelmingly unskilled, and the vast majority of the population remains dependent on subsistence agriculture for economic survival. While GDP growth was estimated at 7% in 2012 and is expected to remain around that level in 2013, it has been driven mostly by high mineral commodity prices and resulting wealth has not generally been shared by the broader population. The reestablishment of relations with international financial institutions such as the International Monetary Fund (IMF) and World Bank after the 1998-2003 war has helped stabilize DRC's macroeconomic situation, but in 2012, the IMF suspended payments under a previous concessional loan agreement due to concerns about a lack of transparency in mining contracts (see "The Mining Sector").

Outside of major cities and industrial mining, economic activity is often carried out within a broad informal sector. The government is trying to improve its business climate, instituting a value-added tax (VAT) in January 2012 to raise revenue. It also joined the Organization for the Harmonization of Business Laws in Africa in August 2012 to simplify and standardize its business regulations. However, it is unclear how equitable collection of the VAT will be, and the DRC is ranked 181 out of 185 countries in the World Bank's 2013 Doing Business Report. The State Department has reported on a number of obstacles to foreign investment and private sector development, including underdeveloped infrastructure, inadequate contract enforcement, limited access to credit, continued insecurity in the east, inadequate property rights protection, high levels of bureaucracy and corruption, and the lack of reliable electricity.[37] In addition, current law requires that Congolese have a majority stake in all agriculture investments, which is seen as a significant impediment to foreign investment in that sector. The DRC government has said it plans to revise the agriculture code and limit the domestic ownership provision.[38]

DRC's sovereign debt declined from 136% of GDP in 2009 to around 25% at the end of 2012, after the country qualified in 2010 for multilateral debt relief worth $12.3 billion under the World Bank- and IMF-led Heavily Indebted Poor Countries (HIPC) initiative.[39] Conditions for the debt cancellation included "satisfactory implementation of the country's poverty reduction and growth strategy, maintenance of macroeconomic stability, improvements in public expenditure and debt management, and improved governance and service delivery in key social sectors, such as health, education and rural development." While macroeconomic progress did occur, analysts have debated whether the World Bank and IMF moved ahead too quickly, thereby losing policy leverage in the absence of significant advances in governance and the business environment.[40]

The Mining Sector

The issue of "conflict minerals"—that is, ores that, when sold or traded, have reportedly helped to fuel conflict or human rights abuses in DRC—has drawn extensive international attention.[41] Conflict mineral exports are particularly associated with the informal, artisanal mining sector in eastern DRC. The vast majority of state revenues from the mining sector, in contrast, come from industrial, large-scale mining of cobalt and copper in the relatively stable Katanga region, in which the mining parastatal Gécamines is a partner. DRC accounts for 47% of the world's cobalt reserves and produced 51% of the world's supply of cobalt in 2010, along with 25% of industrial diamonds, 14% of tantalum, 5% of gem-quality diamonds, and 3% of copper and tin.[42] China has a growing stake in DRC mining: nearly 50% of DRC exports are destined for China, up from 10% in 2005, reportedly including over 90% of mineral exports from Katanga province.[43]

International concerns related to this formal mining sector have focused on corruption, mismanagement, poorly protected property rights, regulatory uncertainty, and, to some extent, poor labor conditions. An independent investigation into five mining concessions sold between 2010 and 2012, for example, reported that DRC lost at least $1.36 billion from underpricing those assets in complex deals featuring offshore companies and two multinational mining corporations, Glencore and the Eurasian Natural Resources Corporation (ENRC). Intermediary companies involved in the deals have been linked to companies owned by Dan Gertler, an Israeli businessman with reportedly close ties to President Kabila.[44]

In December 2012, the IMF halted its concessional lending program in DRC—with a reported $240 million in the pipeline—because DRC had failed to publish mining contracts as required under the program. On April 17, 2013, the Extractive Industries Transparency Initiative (EITI), a U.S.-backed global standard that promotes revenue transparency for extractive resources, suspended the DRC as an EITI candidate country due to the unreliability of the revenue figures it disclosed from its extractive sectors.[45] Similar transparency concerns have been raised concerning DRC's nascent oil sector, although it is still in the exploration phase.[46]

The DRC government has announced plans to revise its mining code. This could allow the state to derive a higher share of mining revenues from the private sector and could, potentially, institute greater transparency. In addition to an increase in royalty payments, draft legislation reportedly includes provisions to increase taxes on mining firms, reduce a 10-year stability clause that shields firms from changes in laws, and increase the government's required stake in joint ventures.[47] The initiative has reportedly sparked concerns from international investors.

U.S. POLICY

The Obama Administration states that its policy toward DRC "is focused on developing a nation that is stable and democratic, at peace with its neighbors, extends state authority across its territory, and provides for the basic needs of its citizens."[48] The Administration also indicates that U.S. relations with DRC are "strong," seemingly based on extensive U.S. efforts to improve DRC's stability, and not necessarily on bilateral diplomatic ties.

In a public address on February 11, 2013, then-Assistant Secretary of State for African Affairs Johnnie Carson called for a new "energetic and international effort" toward a "comprehensive" peace settlement.[49] He argued that high-level U.S. engagement was necessary on moral, strategic, and financial grounds, contrasting the humanitarian costs and burden to donors of continued conflict in DRC against the country's enormous economic potential. The speech presaged Feingold's appointment as the U.S. Special Envoy to the Great Lakes region. On July 25, Secretary of State Kerry chaired a ministerial-level meeting of the U.N. Security Council on the Great Lakes region, at which he argued that there is a shared obligation to end the "targeted, grotesque violence" in DRC, referred to peace in the Great Lakes as "a high-level priority for President Obama and for me," and called for "high-level leadership" to implement and enforce the regional Framework Agreement.[50] Secretary Kerry also applauded a World Bank proposal to provide $1 billion to help states in the region provide better health and education, generate more cross-border trade, and fund hydroelectricity projects, in support of the

Agreement.[51] Whether these remarks and the Envoy appointment mark a major departure for U.S. policy, and whether sufficient U.S. resources are available to implement a new policy approach, remains to be seen.

To date, the Administration has sought to address the M23 conflict through increased regional diplomacy, targeted sanctions instituted under Executive Order 13413 (2006) (with designations of the M23 and the FDLR in January 2013), and actions at the U.N. Security Council that aim to support the regional peace process and MONUSCO's ability to protect civilians in the east. Since mid-2012, the Administration has also publicly criticized Rwanda's reported role in supporting the M23. In July 2012, the State Department suspended FY2012 Foreign Military Financing (FMF) assistance for Rwanda, consistent with the FY2012 Consolidated Appropriations Act (P.L. 112-74), which prohibits FMF assistance for Rwanda and Uganda if they are found to support nonstate armed groups in DRC. While the amount of suspended aid was relatively small, it may have emboldened European donors who then suspended a portion of their direct budgetary support to Rwanda. In December 2012, then-Assistant Secretary of State for African Affairs Johnnie Carson testified before Congress that "there is a credible body of evidence that corroborates the assertions of the U.N. group of experts, that the Rwandan government provided significant military and political support to the M23."[52] In July 2013, a State Department spokesperson again alluded to a "credible body of evidence" regarding "support by senior Rwandan officials to the M23 and of Rwandan military personnel in the DRC," and called on Rwanda "to immediately end any support to the M23, withdraw military personnel from eastern DRC, and follow through on its commitments under the [February 2013] framework."[53]

Foreign Assistance

U.S. bilateral aid to DRC totaled over $254 million in FY2012, about 40% of which was for health programs (**Table 1**).[54] U.S. assistance programs also aim to promote democracy and good governance, stabilization and conflict resolution in the east, agricultural development, natural resource management, military professionalism, and basic service delivery. The Administration has requested $236 million in bilateral aid funding for FY2014, which would represent a significant increase compared to nonhumanitarian FY2012 levels of $186 million. (Food aid, not reflected in the FY2014 request, totaled over $68 million in FY2012. The Administration requested $196.9 million for

FY2013, not counting food aid; actual funding figures for FY2013 are not yet available.) In addition to bilateral aid, the United States provides significant financial support to international financial institutions that have given loans, grants, and technical assistance to DRC. The United States is also the largest donor to MONUSCO under the U.N. system of assessed contributions for peacekeeping operations (**Table 2**).

Table 1. U.S. Bilateral Assistance to DRC, State Department and USAID Appropriations, $ Millions

Account/Fiscal Year	2010 Actual	2011 Actual	2012 Actual	2013 Request	2014 Request
GHP-USAID	65.7	86.0	97.9	89.7	122.7
GHP-State	19.6	39.6	13.8	37.2	38.3
ESF	77.6	45.9	47.9	50.1	59.9
INCLE	1.7	6.0	6.0	5.3	3.3
NADR	0.8	1.0	1.0	0.5	0.5
IMET	0.5	0.5	0.5	0.4	0.3
FMF	1.5	0.3	-	0.2	-
PKO	14.0	21.5	19.0	15.0	11.0
FFP (P.L. 480 Title II)	101.3	67.3	68.3	30.0	-
Subtotal	**282.7**	**268.2**	**254.4**	**228.4**	**236.0**
Add'l Emergency Humanitarian Aid	60.3	57.6	78.6	139.5	-
TOTAL	**343.0**	**325.8**	**333.0**	**367.9**	**236.0**

Source: State Department Congressional Budget Justification for Foreign Operations, FY2012-FY2014; USAID fact-sheets on humanitarian aid to DRC.

Note: The FY2013 column shows the amount allocated as of July 2013 for additional humanitarian assistance. FY2014 figures do not include emergency humanitarian assistance, which is determined during the year according to need. This table does not include funding administered by agencies and departments other than the State Department and USAID, or regional program funding from which DRC may benefit. Totals may not add up due to rounding.

ESF-Economic Support Fund; FFP-Food For Peace; FMF-Foreign Military Financing; GHP-Global Health Programs; IMET- International Military Education & Training; INCLE-International Narcotics Control & Law Enforcement; NADR- Nonproliferation, Antiterrorism, Demining & Related Programs; PKO-Peacekeeping Operations. Additional humanitarian assistance reflects funding administered by USAID's Office of U.S. Foreign Disaster Assistance (OFDA) and the Department of State's Bureau of Population, Refugees, and Migration (PRM), and, for FY2013, emergency FFP aid.

Security assistance is focused on military professionalization and security sector reform. Such aid has largely been funded through the State Department-administered Peacekeeping Operations (PKO) account and has supported officer training, military justice assistance, and efforts to provide better food supplies for troops, among other activities. (U.S. assessed contributions to MONUSCO's budget are funded through a separate account: Contributions to International Peacekeeping, or CIPA.) State Department-administered programs funded through the International Narcotics Control and Law Enforcement (INCLE) account have also supported police professionalization. The Defense Department has also administered some security cooperation programs, such as the Defense Institutions Reform Initiative (DIRI), which assists reforms at the Ministry of Defense. Foreign Military Financing (FMF) funding for DRC, which was relatively small, is prohibited under the Child Soldiers Prevention Act of 2008 (Title IV, P.L. 110-457) and the Victims of Trafficking and Violence Protection Act of 2000 (P.L. 106-386). The Obama Administration has waived such sanctions on other forms of security assistance.[55]

In 2010, State Department-funded contractors and military personnel from U.S. Africa Command (AFRICOM) trained and provided nonlethal equipment to a "model" military battalion, now known as the 391st, using about $35 million in PKO funding. The battalion continued to receive U.S. advisory support, including training on human rights and gender-based violence prevention, until March 2013. At that point, U.S. support was suspended after a U.N. investigation found that members of the 391st, among others, had allegedly raped civilians near Goma during the M23 seizure of the town. Until then, the Administration had been exploring the possibility of training a second battalion; prospects for future U.S.-funded train-and-equip missions are now uncertain.

Table 2. U.S. Contributions to MONUSCO By U.S. Fiscal Year Appropriations, $ Millions

	FY2010	FY2011	FY2012	FY2013 (est.)	FY2014 (req.)
CIPA	387.7	600.2	399.5	408.0	438.0

Source: Congressional Budget Justification, Department of State Operations, FY2012-FY2014.

Note: CIPA=Contributions to International Peacekeeping Activities.

Trade and Investment Issues

With its significant mineral wealth and large domestic market, DRC is potentially an attractive destination for U.S. commerce and investment. A bilateral investment treaty entered into force in 1989, and the Kabila government has taken some steps to improve the country's business climate. However, investors continue to face serious obstacles, as noted above. The State Department also criticized a government review of mining contracts, initiated in 2007, for opacity and delays.[56] The Obama Administration revoked DRC's eligibility for trade benefits under the African Growth and Opportunity Act in December 2010, citing a lack of "continual progress in meeting the requirements" of the act.[57] Bilateral trade is relatively limited; in 2011, U.S. general imports from DRC were valued at $606 million and U.S. exports to DRC at $166 million.[58] In 2012, U.S. imports from DRC fell to $41 million; exports rose to $199 million. Among U.S.-listed companies potentially affected by the 2012 SEC rule regarding the trade in conflict minerals, required under **P.L. 111-203**, some are participating in industry-led initiatives to improve supply- chain accountability, and some are challenging the regulations in court and/or through advocacy.

OUTLOOK AND ISSUES FOR CONGRESS

Through legislation and oversight activities, Members of Congress have expressed an interest in advancing peace and stability, improving governance and natural resource management, and addressing health and humanitarian needs in DRC. However, Congolese political actors have, at times, displayed limited ability and will to pursue such ends. U.S. influence may furthermore be constrained by potential limits on U.S. fiscal and personnel resources, and by the challenges of coordinating with other key players such as European states, China, Rwanda, Uganda, Angola, and South Africa.[59] U.S. bilateral aid does not easily present opportunities for leverage, as most programming is aimed at addressing humanitarian and/or human rights problems. Citing this emphasis, President Obama has waived most legal restrictions on military aid stemming from human rights concerns, using waiver authorities provided by Congress.

The problematic 2011 elections and the renewed rebellion in North Kivu point to the stark obstacles that persist despite international efforts to support post-conflict stabilization and democratic progress. U.S. officials publicly criticized the 2011 electoral process, but in the end, the Obama Administration tacitly accepted Kabila's victory.[60] Some critics of U.S. policy contend that U.S. officials support Kabila because they view him as an anchor of regional stability, whereas—these critics argue—he has failed to improve the lives of most Congolese.[61] Whether or not this criticism is fair, perceptions that the United States is a nonneutral actor in DRC may hinder U.S. diplomatic and foreign assistance efforts. Contrary to some predictions, the disputed election did not lead to a popular uprising and/or mass violence in Kinshasa (to date), but the prospects for improvements in future elections and democratic accountability are uncertain.

With regard to the situation in the Kivus, U.S. policymakers, including in Congress, face a particularly thorny set of challenges. The transfer of M23 faction leader Bosco Ntaganda to the International Criminal Court in March 2013, which the Obama Administration facilitated, may lead to human rights improvements but does not address the root causes of the conflict. The U.N.-backed Framework Agreement between DRC and its neighbors represents a potential step toward more functional regional relationships and a commitment by the DRC government to implement reforms. However, the mechanisms through which it will be implemented and enforced remain to be determined and tested. U.S. and other donor support for security sector reform in DRC has had limited impact on deep structural problems, in part due to seemingly low DRC government interest in restructuring a security apparatus whose dysfunction may benefit powerful actors. Cyclical conflict in the east also continues to highlight challenges confronted by MONUSCO, whose mandate and capabilities have often appeared to diverge. Whether the authorization of MONUSCO's new Intervention Brigade will close that gap, or increase it, is uncertain.

A key issue for Congress is whether a focus on issues such as sexual violence and the trade in conflict minerals has distracted from systemic governance problems—or has resulted in a policy that overwhelmingly concentrates on the east at the possible expense of the rest of the country. Debate continues among policymakers in Congress and the executive branch over issues such as:

- the strategic design of U.S. aid to DRC, such as whether aid flows to the areas of greatest need and/or highest U.S. national interests, and its impact;

- the degree to which U.S. aid to DRC and neighboring states can or should be conditioned or restricted as a tool of policy leverage;
- the relative effectiveness of various tools for exerting U.S. influence, such as diplomacy, foreign assistance programming, U.S. influence over international financial institution activities, and U.S. actions at the U.N. Security Council; and
- the degree to which the Kabila government has shown progress, even when assisted and prodded by donors, in confronting deeply ingrained problems related to the security sector, economic governance, and state accountability and capacity.

APPENDIX. SELECTED ENACTED LEGISLATION

- **P.L. 109-456 (Sen. Barack Obama), Democratic Republic of the Congo Relief, Security, and Democracy Promotion Act of 2006** (December 22, 2006). Sought to define U.S. policy toward DRC. Obligated a minimum funding level for bilateral foreign assistance to DRC in FY2006-FY2007, authorized the Secretary of State to withhold certain types of foreign assistance for countries acting to destabilize DRC, and directed the President to consider withdrawing certain forms of aid to DRC if the government did not make sufficient progress toward stated policy objectives.
- **P.L. 110-457 (Rep. Howard L. Berman), William Wilberforce Trafficking Victims Protection Reauthorization Act of 2008** (December 23, 2008). Prohibits, with certain waiver provisions, certain security assistance funds and military sales from being made available to the government of a country identified by the Secretary of State as supporting the recruitment and use of child soldiers, and (pursuant to P.L. 106-386) to countries that receive a Tier 3 (worst) ranking in the State Department's annual *Trafficking in Persons Report*.
- **P.L. 111-32 (Rep. David R. Obey), Supplemental Appropriations Act, 2009** (June 24, 2009). Appropriated $15 million in Peacekeeping Operations (PKO) funding for DRC that was used to train a Light Infantry Battalion, as part of ongoing U.S. support for security sector reform.

- **P.L. 111-84 (Rep. Ike Skelton), National Defense Authorization Act for Fiscal Year 2010** (October 28, 2009). Required the executive branch to produce a map of mineral-rich areas under the control of armed groups in DRC.
- **P.L. 111-172 (Sen. Russ Feingold), Lord's Resistance Army Disarmament and Northern Uganda Recovery Act** (May 24, 2010). Directed the President to submit to Congress a strategy to guide U.S. support for efforts to eliminate the threat to civilians and regional stability posed by the Lord's Resistance Army (LRA)—an armed group originating in Uganda and currently active in DRC and other central African countries—among other provisions.
- **P.L. 111-203 (Rep. Barney Frank), Dodd-Frank Wall Street Reform and Consumer Protection Act** (July 21, 2010). Required the Securities and Exchange Commission to issue regulations requiring U.S.-listed companies whose products rely on certain designated "conflict minerals" to disclose whether such minerals originated in DRC or adjoining countries and to describe related due diligence measures, along with a number of other provisions.
- **P.L. 111-212 (Rep. David Obey), Supplemental Appropriations Act, 2010** (July 29, 2010). Appropriated $15 million in Economic Support Fund (ESF) to assist emergency security and humanitarian assistance for civilians, particularly women and girls, in eastern DRC.
- **P.L. 112-10 (Rep. Harold Rogers), Department of Defense and Full-Year Continuing Appropriations Act, 2011** (April 15, 2011). Provided that certain military assistance funds available for DRC should not be used to support any military training or operations that "include child soldiers."
- **P.L. 112-74 (Rep. John Abney Culberson), Consolidated Appropriations Act, 2012** (December 23, 2011). As amended and extended to FY2013 through continuing resolutions, prohibits certain types of security assistance and arms sales to DRC for training or operations that include child soldiers. Restricts Foreign Military Financing (FMF) grants to Rwanda and Uganda if the Secretary of State finds that these countries are providing support to armed groups in DRC. Previous annual foreign operations appropriations bills placed reporting requirements and restrictions on the allocation of FMF and International Military Education and Training (IMET) funds for DRC.

- **P.L. 112-239 (Rep. Howard "Buck" McKeon), National Defense Authorization Act, 2013** (January 2, 2013). Authorizes sanctions on individuals found to have provided significant support to the M23.

End Notes

[1] Net flows of official development assistance (ODA), Organization for Economic Cooperation and Development (OECD); GDP, International Monetary Fund (IMF) World Economic Outlook database, April 2013.

[2] In 2006 (latest available), the World Bank estimated that over 95% of the population lived on less than $2 a day. Note that statistical data used in this report are often approximate, as authoritative data from DRC are generally lacking.

[3] DRC also hosts some 179,000 refugees, predominately from Angola, Rwanda, and the Central African Republic.

[4] United Nations, *An Overview of Global Humanitarian Action at Mid-Year*, 2013.

[5] Katanga was the heart of the colonial mining industry and continues to be the center of industrial mining, the main engine of DRC's economy. It has also been the seat of multiple separatist rebellions. In February 2013, the U.N. Office for the Coordination of Humanitarian Affairs (UNOCHA) reported that armed group activity in Katanga had provoked "an acute humanitarian crisis" and caused over 300,000 people to be internally displaced.

[6] MONUSCO is currently the second-largest U.N. peacekeeping operation (after Darfur) in number of troops, but others are much larger compared to local population size, such as those in Côte d'Ivoire, Haiti, Lebanon, Liberia, and South Sudan. (See U.N. Peacekeeping Fact Sheet: http://www.un.org/en/peacekeeping/resources.

[7] See CRS Report R42618, *Conflict Minerals in Central Africa: U.S. and International Responses*, by Nicolas Cook.

[8] The LRA is a small militia of Ugandan origin, currently present in DRC, the Central African Republic, South Sudan, and possibly Sudan. LRA massacres, mass abductions, sexual assault, and looting have caused significant human suffering and instability. The Ugandan military, or UPDF, deployed to DRC for counter-LRA operations in late 2008, with significant U.S. logistical support. However, most Ugandan troops withdrew from DRC in 2011 after the DRC government and military leaders objected to their continued presence. The UPDF reportedly retains a small presence at a U.N. logistics hub for counter-LRA operations in Dungu, northeastern DRC.

[9] State Department, "Press Briefing Announcement Regarding Great Lakes Special Representative," June 18, 2013.

[10] See CRS Report R42497, *Trafficking in Persons: International Dimensions and Foreign Policy Issues for Congress*, by Liana Sun Wyler.

[11] For analysis of these events, see Adam Hochschild, *King Leopold's Ghost*, Mariner Books: 2006.

[12] Some analysts have accused the United States of covert involvement in the Lumumba assassination. A 1975 congressional investigation into alleged U.S. foreign assassination plots concluded that the Central Intelligence Agency (CIA) had pursued plans to assassinate Lumumba, a populist who received support from the Soviet Union, but that they were thwarted by logistical factors. The investigation further concluded that available evidence did not point to a direct CIA role in Lumumba's death, despite advance CIA knowledge that Lumumba would likely be killed in the way that he was. See *Alleged Assassination Plots*

Involving Foreign Leaders: An Interim Report of the Select Committee to Study Government Operations with Respect to Intelligence Activities, U.S. Senate, November 20, 1975; pp. 30, 48. The ad- hoc congressional committee was commonly referred to as the Church Committee after its chairman, Senator Frank Church. See also Lawrence Devlin, *Chief of Station, Congo*, PublicAffairs: 2008.

[13] Notably, Mobutu's government reportedly served as a conduit for U.S. assistance to anti-government rebels in neighboring Angola. See, e.g., John Stockwell, *In Search Of Enemies*, New York: Norton, 1979; and Howard W. French, "Anatomy of an Autocracy: Mobutu's 32-Year Reign," *New York Times*, May 17, 1997.

[14] See, e.g., Steve Askin and Carole Collins, "External Collusion with Kleptocracy: Can Zaïre Recapture Its Stolen Wealth?" *Review of African Political Economy*, 57 (1993). For further analysis of the Mobutu era, see Library of Congress, Federal Research Division, *Zaire: A Country Study*, 1994, at http://lcweb2.loc.gov/frd/cs/zrtoc.html.

[15] For a detailed account of the second Congo conflict and events preceding it, see Jason Stearns, *Dancing in the Glory of Monsters: The Collapse of the Congo and the Great War of Africa*, PublicAffairs: 2011.

[16] See Thomas Turner, *The Congo Wars: Conflict, Myth and Reality*, Zed Books: 2007; Gérard Prunier, *Africa's World War: Congo, The Rwandan Genocide, and the Making of a Continental Catastrophe*, Oxford University Press: 2008; René Lemarchand, *The Dynamics of Violence in Central Africa*, University of Pennsylvania Press: 2009; Howard W. French, "Kagame's Hidden War in the Congo," *New York Review of Books*, September 24, 2009; and Stearns, op.cit.

[17] Most independent observers assert that the FDLR's ranks have drastically diminished over the past decade. Still, insecurity in North Kivu could create opportunities for the FDLR to regroup, and Rwanda claimed a series of FDLR attacks on its territory in late 2012. See *Report of the Secretary-General on the United Nations Organization Stabilization Mission in the Democratic Republic of the Congo*, November 14, 2012, U.N. doc. S/2012/838.

[18] On alleged Rwandan smuggling during the 1998-2003 war, see *Report of the Panel of Experts on the Illegal Exploitation of Natural Resources and Other Forms of Wealth of the Democratic Republic of the Congo*, April 2001, U.N. doc. S/2001/357; on more recent periods, see Howard French, 2009, op. cit.

[19] See, e.g., European Union Election Observation Mission in the DRC, "Elections Présidentielle, Législatives et Provinciales 2006, Rapport Final," February 23, 2007.

[20] Carter Center, "DRC Presidential Election Results Lack Credibility," December 10, 2011; European Union, "The Election Observation Mission of the European Union Deplores The Lack Of Transparency And Irregularities In The Collection, Compilation And Publication Of Results," December 13, 2011; *Direct.cd*, "'Résultats conformes ni à la vérité ni à la justice,' affirme Monsengwo," December 12, 2011; International Crisis Group (ICG), *Congo: The Electoral Dilemma*, May 5, 2011; and *Report of the United Nations Joint Human Rights Office on Serious Human Rights Violations Committed by Members of the Congolese Defense and Security Forces [...] Between 26 November and 25 December 2011*, March 2012. Regional observers, on the other hand, largely praised the election; see "Joint Statement by the AU, SADC, ECCAS, ICGLR, and Comesa, on the General Elections in the Democratic Republic of Congo," November 30, 2011.

[21] Carter Center, "Democratic Republic of the Congo Legislative Election Results Compromised," February 23, 2012; e.g., statement of Mvemba Phezo Dizolele before the Senate Foreign Relations Committee, December 15, 2011.

[22] See, e.g., *Africa Confidential*, "Congo-Kinshasa: The Real Power Politics," June 21, 2013.

[23] See, e.g., USAID Fact Sheet, *Democratic Republic of the Congo – Complex Emergency*, June 28, 2013; and Adam Nossiter, "For Congo Children, Food Today Means None Tomorrow," *New York Times*, January 2, 2012.

[24] See, among others, State Department, *Country Reports on Human Rights Practices for 2012, 2013; Report of the Secretary-General on the Implementation of Security Council*

Resolutions 1820 (2008) and 1888 (2009), November 24, 2010, U.N. document A/65/592–S/2010/604; and Human Rights Watch (HRW), *Soldiers Who Rape, Commanders Who Condone: Sexual Violence and Military Reform in the Democratic Republic of Congo*, July 16, 2009.

[25] The mutiny followed threats by President Kabila to arrest ex-CNDP commander Bosco Ntaganda and efforts to break up and redeploy ex-CNDP units outside the Kivu region, their ethnic and economic stronghold. Ntaganda, who had been integrated into the DRC military in 2009 with the rank of General, had been subject to an International Criminal Court (ICC) arrest warrant since 2006 in connection with crimes allegedly committed in the adjacent northern Ituri district. In March 2013, following a split in the M23, he turned himself in to the U.S. Embassy in neighboring Rwanda and reportedly requested to be transferred to the ICC, which the United States facilitated. He is now awaiting trial. The American Servicemembers' Protection Act (ASPA; Title II, P.L. 107-206) limits U.S. support for the ICC; the Obama Administration appears to have interpreted diplomatic support and information sharing, including Ntaganda's transfer, as permitted. Administration officials had previously called for Ntaganda's arrest.

[26] Established in 2003, the U.N. sanctions regime in DRC consists of an arms embargo against armed groups in the country that are not part of the Government's integrated army or police units, as well as a travel ban and an asset freeze on violators of the embargo and other designated persons and entities, as determined by Security Council resolutions. U.N. doc. S/2012/348/Add.1, June 27, 2012; U.N. doc. S/2012/843, November 15, 2012; and U.N. doc. S/AC.43/2012/NOTE.26, November 26, 2012.

[27] *BBC News*, "DR Congo's M23 rebels: Rwandan Support 'falling,'" July 5, 2013.

[28] The U.N. Secretary-General, African Union (AU), Southern African Development Community (SADC), and the International Conference on the Great Lakes Region signed as witnesses to the agreement.

[29] Jason Stearns, "Next Challenge for Congo: International Terrorism," *Christian Science Monitor/Africa Monitor*, July 28, 2010. Other analysts, however, assert that "the group's allegiance to Islamism seems rather superficial." See ICG, *Eastern Congo: The ADF-NALU's Lost Rebellion*, December 19, 2012. In July 2013, ADF attacks in North Kivu resulted in significant population displacements, according to news reports.

[30] USAID Factsheet, *Democratic Republic of the Congo – Complex Emergency*, June 28, 2013.

[31] Welthungerhilfe, Concern Worldwide, and International Food Policy Research Institute (IFPRI), "2011 Global Hunger Index, The Challenge of Hunger: Taming Price Spikes and Excessive Food Price Volatility," October 2011. Note: DRC was not ranked in the 2012 index due to insufficient available data.

[32] State Department, *Country Reports for Human Rights Practices for 2012*, op. cit.

[33] Harvard Humanitarian Initiative, *Characterizing Sexual Violence in the Democratic Republic of the Congo*, 2009. See CRS Report R40956, Sexual Violence in African Conflicts, by Alexis Arieff.

[34] HRW, *Soldiers Who Rape, Commanders Who Condone*, 2009, op. cit.

[35] United Nations Conduct and Discipline Unit, "Statistics," June 19, 2013

[36] ICG, *Congo: The Electoral Dilemma*, 2011, op. cit.

[37] State Department, "Investment Climate Statement-2013," April 2013.

[38] Michael Kavanagh, "Congo Seeks to Lure Investors for $5.7 Billion Farming Plan," *Bloomberg News*, July 12, 2013.

[39] IMF, *Democratic Republic of the Congo Staff Report for the 2012 Article IV Consultation*, September 4, 2012; and "IMF and World Bank Announce US$12.3 Billion in Debt Relief for the Democratic Republic of the Congo," July 1, 2010. This was the largest amount of debt relief provided to any eligible HIPC country, according to the IMF.

[40] See, e.g., Oxford Analytica, "Relief for Congo," July 7, 2010.

[41] See CRS Report R42618, *Conflict Minerals in Central Africa: U.S. and International Responses*, by Nicolas Cook.

[42] *Extractive Industries Transparency Initiative (EITI)*, "Democratic Republic of Congo: Overview."

[43] IMF Trade Data; *Economist Intelligence Unit*, "Congo (Democratic Republic)," June 11, 2013.

[44] See, for example, Franz Wild, Michael J. Kavanagh, and Jonathan Ferziger, "Gertler Earns Millions as Mine Deals Fail to Enrich Congo," *Bloomberg Markets Magazine*, December 5, 2012; *Africa Confidential*, "Gertler's Assets Multiply," May 24, 2013; and Africa Progress Panel Report 2013, *Equity in Extractives*, May 2013, which point to the systematic under-valuing of state-controlled mining assets sold to private foreign investors.

[45] EITI, "Democratic Republic of Congo Temporarily 'Suspended,'" April 18, 2013; see also EITI, *République Démocratique du Congo: Report 2010*, December 2012.

[46] See ICG, *Black Gold in the Congo: Threat to Stability or Development Opportunity?* July 11, 2012. Oil deposits have recently been found on the Ugandan side of Lake Albert, which also borders DRC, and Angola exports oil from offshore deposits bordering DRC.

[47] *Africa Mining Intelligence*, "Outcry Over New Mining Legislation," May 14, 2013.

[48] State Department, "U.S. Relations with Democratic Republic of the Congo," December 3, 2012.

[49] Remarks at the Brookings Institution, "Finding a Lasting Solution to Instability in the Democratic Republic of the Congo," February 11, 2013.

[50] John Kerry, "Remarks at the United Nations Security Council Ministerial on the Great Lakes," July 25, 2013.

[51] See World Bank, "World Bank Announces US$1 Billion Pledge to Africa's Great Lakes Region," May 22, 2013.

[52] Testimony before the House Foreign Affairs Committee, Subcommittee on Africa, Global Health, and Human Rights, December 11, 2012; and before the House Armed Services Committee, December 19, 2012.

[53] State Department daily press briefing, July 23, 2013.

[54] State Department, FY2014 *Congressional Budget Justification for Foreign Operations*.

[55] See Presidential Determination 2012-16 with Respect to Foreign Governments' Efforts Regarding Trafficking in Persons, September 14, 2012; and Presidential Determination No. 2012-18 of September 28, 2012, with respect to the Child Soldiers Prevention Act of 2008.

[56] State Department, "Background Note: Congo (Kinshasa)," April 13, 2011.

[57] "Presidential Proclamation—African Growth and Opportunity Act," December 21, 2010.

[58] U.S. International Trade Commission data, accessed at http://dataweb.usitc.gov/scripts

[59] South Africa in particular has recently elevated its influence in DRC, providing the bulk of troops for the U.N. Intervention Brigade and committing to purchase a sizable share of energy production from the prospective DRC Grand Inga III dam. South African relations with Rwanda also appear to have deteriorated due to a range of factors.

[60] State Department, Press Statement, Hillary Rodham Clinton, "Supreme Court Decision Confirming Results of the Presidential Election in the Democratic Republic of the Congo (DRC)," December 20, 2011.

[61] See, e.g., testimony by Mvemba Phezo Dizolele before the Senate Committee on Foreign Relations, 2011, op. cit.

In: Democratic Republic of Congo
Editor: Shelby Rake

ISBN: 978-1-63117-544-2
© 2014 Nova Science Publishers, Inc.

Chapter 2

DEMOCRATIC REPUBLIC OF THE CONGO 2012 HUMAN RIGHTS REPORT[*]

U.S. Department of State; Bureau of Democracy, Human Rights and Labor

EXECUTIVE SUMMARY

The Democratic Republic of the Congo (DRC) is a nominally centralized, constitutional republic. The president and the lower house of parliament (National Assembly) are popularly elected. Provincial assemblies choose the members of the upper house (Senate). In November 2011 the country held multiparty presidential and National Assembly elections, which many local and international observers judged lacked credibility and were seriously flawed. There were many instances in which state security forces (SSF) acted independently of civilian control and of military command.

Weak civilian control over SSF contributed to increased conflict in eastern Congo. In April integrated former rebels of the National Congress for the Defense of the People (CNDP) defected from the national army (FARDC). Subsequently, they created the M23 armed group (named after the March 23,

---

[*] This is an edited, reformatted and augmented version of a report released by the U.S. Department of State; Bureau of Democracy, Human Rights and Labor, dated April 2013.

2009, peace agreements) and challenged government control in the eastern part of the country, which led to violence, the displacement of large numbers of persons, and significant human rights abuses, including the M23's recruitment and use of children in armed conflict. During the year the government entered into a UN-backed action plan to end the recruitment and use of child soldiers, and the government made significant improvements to reduce the presence of children in the nation's armed forces.

The three most important human rights issues were: armed conflict in the East that exacerbated an already precarious human rights situation, particularly with regard to sexual- and gender-based violence (SGBV); the lack of an independent and effective judiciary; and impunity throughout the country for many serious abuses, including unlawful killings, disappearances, torture, rape, and arbitrary arrests and detention.

Other major human rights problems included the following: severe and life- threatening conditions in prison and detention facilities; prolonged pretrial detention; arbitrary interference with privacy, family, and home; SSF members abusing, threatening, and obstructing journalists, human rights advocates, and the work of UN investigators; abuse of internally displaced persons (IDPs) by SSF and rebel and militia groups (RMG); widespread official corruption; SSF and RMG retention and recruitment of child soldiers; and use of forced civilian labor. Societal discrimination and abuse, particularly against women, children, persons with disabilities, as well as lesbian, gay, bisexual, and transgender (LGBT) persons, and persons with albinism; enslavement of Pygmies; trafficking in persons; child labor; and lack of protection of workers' rights were also problems.

Despite some modest improvements, impunity for human rights abuses remained a severe problem in the security services. Authorities did not prosecute or punish the great majority of abusers.

RMG, some of which were supported by foreign governments and militaries, committed violent abuses against civilians, particularly in North Kivu, South Kivu, and Orientale provinces. The abuses--some of which may constitute war crimes-- included unlawful killings, disappearances, torture, and SGBV. RMG also recruited, abducted, and retained child soldiers and compelled forced labor. RMG and some army units engaged in the illegal exploitation and trade of natural resources in the East. In a separate conflict in the Haut Uele and Bas Uele districts of Orientale Province, the Lord's Resistance Army (LRA) continued to commit serious human rights violations through attacks resulting in deaths, injuries, abductions, forced labor, looting, and general insecurity.

SECTION 1. RESPECT FOR THE INTEGRITY OF THE PERSON, INCLUDING FREEDOM FROM

a. Arbitrary or Unlawful Deprivation of Life

On several occasions during the year, SSF members arbitrarily and unlawfully killed civilians, sometimes during apprehension or while holding them in custody. For example, on February 16 in Lubero Territory, North Kivu, a man who was accused of killing a FARDC officer was killed in retaliation by another FARDC officer.

The FARDC and RMG, a number of which included FARDC defectors who had previously been integrated into the army following 2009 peace agreements, were responsible for politically motivated killings, arbitrary arrests, temporary detentions, and the abduction and disappearance of many individuals.

Human Rights Watch (HRW) reported in December 2011 that SSF killed 24 individuals, including bystanders and members of the opposition, in elections- related violence on December 9-14, 2011. In March the UN published its report of human rights violations in Kinshasa during the elections period, stating that SSF had killed 33 individuals. In response, the government issued its own report, attributing 20 elections-related killings to SSF in Kinshasa. At year's end these killings remained under investigation.

On June 19, the courts opened the appeal process related to the 2010 killing of human rights activist Floribert Chebeya and his driver. In 2011 the civil party representing the families of the deceased claimed only "partial satisfaction" with the verdict and filed an appeal calling for former National Police (PNC) Inspector General John Numbi to be tried. On October 23, the high military court dismissed the case against Numbi but decided to investigate the assertions of Paul Mwilambwe, an absconded police officer who claimed to know the location of the body of Chebeya's driver.

RMG in conflict zones committed unlawful killings (see section 1.g.).

b. Disappearance

There were reports of disappearances attributable to SSF. Authorities often refused to acknowledge the detention of suspects and in some cases detained suspects in unofficial facilities. For example, Eugene Diomi, a national deputy, disappeared on June 27, and upon his release on October 10, reported that the PNC had detained him and moved him multiple times during his detention. Diomi claimed he was targeted for publicly supporting the opposition and denied that his detention was related to the warrant for his arrest for allegedly raping two minor girls. As a member of parliament, Diomi holds immunities and privileges, which parliament had not waived at year's end.

RMG and some FARDC elements kidnapped numerous persons, generally for forced labor, military service, or sexual services. Many of these victims disappeared (see section 1.g.).

c. Torture and Other Cruel, Inhuman, or Degrading Treatment or Punishment

A 2011 law criminalizes torture, and in July the government began a campaign to educate SSF and the population on this year-old law. Nevertheless, there were reports from human rights organizations that SSF continued to torture civilians, particularly detainees and prisoners, and employed other types of cruel, inhuman, and degrading punishment. There were some reports of government authorities taking action against persons responsible for these acts.

A number of organizations documented cases of torture. For example, the Center for Research on the Environment, Democracy, and Human Rights reported that on January 15, Bienfait Magambo died after he was kidnapped and tortured for hours near Goma by a FARDC unit reporting to Seraphin Mirindi. Mirindi later deserted and joined the M23 rebel group.

On several occasions during the year, SSF utilized cruel, inhuman, or degrading methods to exact punishment. For example, on May 8 in Kalemie Territory, Katanga, a man was arrested by police officers after not responding to a summons, bound, and left in the sun for several hours. He was then trampled by civilians before being released that same day. The public prosecutor issued an arrest warrant against those believed to be responsible.

In addition there were several reports during the year that SSF harassed and arrested journalists who wrote or broadcast material SSF deemed critical of the government and inappropriate due to the conflict in eastern Congo (see section 2.a.).

Some church leaders and family or community members also beat, starved, and abandoned children accused of witchcraft (see section 6).

There were continuing reports, including many from the UN's Joint Human Rights Office (UNJHRO), of members of the SSF and RMG raping civilians, both in the conflict zone in the East (see section 1.g.) and elsewhere.

Prison and Detention Center Conditions

Conditions in most prisons remained severe and life threatening. The penal system was underfunded, and most prisons were understaffed, undersupplied, overcrowded, and poorly maintained. Serious threats to life and health were widespread and included violence, particularly rape; food shortages; and inadequate food, potable water, space, sanitation, ventilation, temperature control, lighting, and medical care. Death from starvation or disease was not uncommon. Men and women, juveniles and adults, and pretrial detainees and convicted prisoners were often held together. Escapes were common.

Physical Conditions: According to the Joint Prison Coordination (which comprises the Ministry of Justice, the Ministry of Defense, and UN Stabilization Mission in the DRC (MONUSCO)), in 2010 (the latest information available) the number of persons in pretrial detention exceeded 18,000, including an estimated 500 women.

The reported total number of sentenced prisoners did not exceed 4,000, including approximately 100 women. These figures represent several times the number of persons the system was designed to hold. For example, while the prison in Bunia was constructed to house 220 inmates, as of September 24, 1,014 individuals were detained there. Of those, 832 were pretrial detainees and 182 were convicted prisoners. Thirty-one women were among the detained as were six children, living with their parents. This prison had three staff members and eight volunteers.

Even harsher conditions prevailed in small detention centers, which were extremely overcrowded; had no toilets, mattresses, or medical care; and provided detainees with insufficient amounts of light, fresh air, and water. Originally intended to house short-term detainees, they were often used for lengthy incarceration. They generally operated without dedicated funding and with minimal regulation or oversight. Prisons are generally run by their directors and staff as profit-making enterprises, wherein sleeping arrangements are sold to the highest bidder and visits are paid for by family members and prisoners. Informed sources stated that detention center authorities often arbitrarily beat or tortured detainees. For example, prison authorities in Goma beat Mumbere Kisuba, who as a result died on January 29.

Despite President Kabila's 2006 decision to close illegal jails operated by the military or other state security forces, there were no reports of such closures during the year. According to MONUSCO, SSF, particularly the intelligence services and the Republican Guard (RG), continued to operate numerous illegal detention facilities characterized by harsh and life-threatening conditions. Authorities routinely denied family members, friends, and lawyers access to these facilities.

Administration: Authorities denied some inmates access to visitors and often did not permit them to have contact with or submit complaints to judicial authorities (see section 1.d.). After the new government took office in late April, it began to regularly inspect detention centers. For instance, 66 inspections were undertaken in 29 detention centers in August. As a result of these inspections, the justice minister referred a number of cases to the general prosecutor, and seven officials and prison directors were arrested. There were no government ombudsmen serving to protect the rights of prisoners and detainees. There were no reports of authorities preventing prisoners or detainees from practicing their religion. Authorities took no meaningful steps to improve recordkeeping or to use alternatives to incarceration for nonviolent offenders. In general the conditions of women prisoners were no worse than those for men.

Monitoring: On most occasions the government allowed the International Committee of the Red Cross, MONUSCO, and nongovernmental organizations (NGOs) access to official detention facilities. However, it did not allow these organizations access to illegal government-run detention facilities.

RMG detained civilians, often for ransom, but little information was available concerning the conditions of detention (see section 1.g.).

d. Arbitrary Arrest or Detention

The law prohibits arbitrary arrest or detention; however, SSF arbitrarily arrested and detained persons on a routine basis.

Role of the Police and Security Apparatus
The PNC operates under the Ministry of Interior and has primary responsibility for law enforcement and public order. The PNC includes the Rapid Intervention Police and the Integrated Police Unit. The National

Intelligence Agency (ANR), overseen by the president's national security advisor, is responsible for internal and external intelligence. Other SSF operating under the control of the Ministry of Defense and primarily responsible for external security, but also fulfilling an internal security role, include the FARDC and the military intelligence service. The presidency oversees the RG, and the minister of interior oversees the Direction Generale de Migration, which is responsible for border control.

Elements of the SSF remained undisciplined and corrupt, and most SSF were undertrained and grossly underfunded, although the situation improved somewhat over the course of the year. The initiative of the European Union Police Mission in the DRC to provide biometric identification cards to the PNC facilitated an unprecedented census of police officers and resulted in some progress toward increased professionalism.

Mechanisms existed to investigate abuses by SSF and address internal discipline problems, although they were weak and ineffective, particularly for addressing misconduct by mid- and high-ranking officials. Some progress was made during the year to reduce impunity within the PNC and FARDC. For example, on July 2, in Mitwaba, Katanga Province, a FARDC officer reportedly ordered the extrajudicial execution of 14 inmates after an attack by the armed group Mai Mai Gedeon. (Six of the victims were allegedly affiliated with Mai Mai Gedeon.). The alleged perpetrators--a captain and five officers--were arrested and prosecuted; the trial continued at year's end.

In 2011 the government adopted a law that reorganizes judicial police and other organs to improve coordination and justice, but implementation was slow. The FARDC suffers from weak command and control, poor operational planning, low administrative and logistical capacity, lack of training, and questionable loyalty of some of its soldiers, particularly those in the East. Other serious obstacles to the formation of a professional national army included lack of equipment and facilities. Beginning in April the FARDC's capabilities were further weakened by the defection of a large number of soldiers in North Kivu, many of whom were ex- CNDP officers who had previously been integrated into the FARDC (see section 1.g.).

PNC and FARDC units throughout the country regularly engaged in illegal taxation and extortion of civilians. They set up checkpoints to collect "taxes," often arresting individuals who could not pay the demanded bribes and stealing food and money. According to UNJHRO there was a direct correlation between the amount siphoned off from SSF personnel salaries and the level of human rights abuses committed by SSF personnel. Abuses by FARDC soldiers were dramatically reduced in areas where they were properly paid and fed.

Impunity in the SSF remained a widespread problem, exacerbated and abetted by the weaknesses of the justice system (see section 1.e.). However, the government increasingly prosecuted and disciplined security force personnel for abusing civilians. Nevertheless, military justice institutions continued to face challenges, such as a severe shortage of military judges and prosecutors. Magistrates, prosecutors, and investigators were poorly trained, had few or no resources for investigations, and had limited access to legal codes. In addition the military justice system was often subjected to political and command interference, and security arrangements for magistrates in conflict-affected areas were inadequate. In some instances magistrates who attempted to investigate politically connected, high-level FARDC officers were threatened, as were witnesses providing information to judicial officers.

The government continued to maintain human rights committees with MONUSCO in several provinces. Depending on the province, the committees were composed of military and police officers, judicial authorities, military prosecutors, MONUSCO human rights officers, and MONUSCO child protection officers. Committees met regularly, normally on a monthly basis, to monitor, investigate, and develop strategies to combat human rights abuses. Some observers claimed the committees produced weak results overall.

Arrest Procedures and Treatment While in Detention

By law arrests for offenses punishable by more than six months' imprisonment require warrants. Detainees must appear before a magistrate within 48 hours. Authorities must inform those arrested of their rights and the reason for their arrest, and they may not arrest a family member instead of the individual being sought. Authorities must allow arrested individuals to contact their families and consult with attorneys. In practice security officials routinely violated all of these requirements. Many detainees were not granted court hearings within the required 48 hours. While the law provides for a bail system, it generally did not function, and detainees who were unable to pay were rarely able to access legal counsel. Authorities often held suspects in incommunicado detention, including in illegal facilities run by the ANR and the RG, and refused to acknowledge these detentions.

Arbitrary Arrest: Security personnel sometimes arrested and detained perceived opponents and critics of the government, occasionally under the pretext of state security, and often denied due process, such as access to an attorney (see sections 1.a., 2.a., and 5). For example, the SSF arrested journalist Pierre-Sosthene Kambidi on August 28 after he reported on the defection of FARDC Colonel John Tshibangu in a manner that some considered unfavorable to the government.

Police sometimes arbitrarily arrested and detained persons without filing charges to extort money from family members or because administrative systems were not well established.

The military intelligence agency, DEMIAP, arbitrarily arrested individuals and subjected them to prolonged arbitrary detention.

Pretrial Detention: Prolonged pretrial detention, often ranging from months to years, remained a problem. Trial delays were due to factors such as judicial inefficiency, administrative obstacles, corruption, financial constraints, and staff shortages. Prison officials often held individuals after their sentences had expired due to disorganization, inadequate records, judicial inefficiency, or corruption. Some prisoners were also unable to pay fines as their sentences required and instead remained in prison indefinitely after they had served their sentences.

e. Denial of Fair Public Trial

While the law provides for an independent judiciary, in practice the judiciary was corrupt and subject to influence. Judges were poorly and irregularly compensated and subject to influence and coercion by officials and other influential individuals. A shortage of judges hindered the government's ability to provide expeditious trials. Further, judges sometimes refused to be transferred to remote areas of the country due to lack of housing and difficult living conditions. Authorities routinely did not respect court orders. Disciplinary boards created under the High Council of Magistrates began ruling on numerous cases of corruption and malpractice each month; many of these rulings included the firing or fining of judges and magistrates.

Trial Procedures

The constitution provides for a presumption of innocence. However, in practice most defendants were assumed guilty and had to prove their innocence. Rarely did a presiding judge require the prosecution to prove its case. Authorities are required to inform the defendant of the charges, including in writing and interpreted as needed. Counsel is not required to be provided in most cases, with the exception of murder trials. While the government regularly provided legal counsel in capital cases, lawyers often did not have adequate access to their clients. During trials defendants have the right to be present and to be represented by a defense attorney.

These rights were occasionally disregarded in practice. Adequate time was generally provided to the defendant to prepare a defense. The country does not use a jury system. The public could attend trials at the discretion of the presiding judge. Defendants have the right to a trial within 15 days of being charged. This time period can be extended to a maximum of 45 days. Authorities only occasionally abided by this requirement. The law requires that defendants have access to government-held evidence, but this right was irregularly observed. Defendants did not regularly exercise their right to confront witnesses against them and to present evidence and witnesses in their own defense because witnesses were often reluctant to testify for fear of retaliation. Defendants are not compelled to testify or confess guilt. Defendants have the right to appeal, except in cases involving national security, armed robbery, and smuggling, which the Court of State Security usually adjudicates.

Political Prisoners and Detainees

There were reports of political prisoners and detainees. Voix des Sans-Voix, a domestic NGO, reported 213 political detainees, approximately the same number as in 2011. While the government permitted access to some of these prisoners by international human rights organizations and MONUSCO, authorities consistently denied access to detention facilities run by the RG and the ANR (see section 1.c.).

Civil Judicial Procedures and Remedies

Individuals can seek civil remedies for human rights violations within the civil court system. However, individuals preferred to seek redress in the criminal courts and rarely utilized civil courts to address human rights violations.

f. Arbitrary Interference with Privacy, Family, Home, or Correspondence

Although the law prohibits arbitrary interference with privacy, family, home, or correspondence, SSF routinely ignored these provisions. SSF harassed and robbed civilians, entered and searched homes and vehicles without warrants, and looted homes, businesses, and schools. Many of those responsible for such acts remained unidentified and unpunished. The most common offense by the FARDC, as documented by the UN for the month of July, was the violation of the right to property, particularly looting.

g. Use of Excessive Force and Other Abuses in Internal Conflicts

Both local and foreign-influenced conflicts continued in mineral-rich parts of the East, particularly in North Kivu and South Kivu, Katanga, Bas Uele and Haut Uele districts of Orientale Province, and to a lesser degree, the Ituri District of Orientale. Conflict, centered around Rutshuru, North Kivu, reignited when former CNDP elements, who had been integrated into the FARDC, began defecting in April and formed the "March 23 Movement," or M23 (which occasionally used the name Congolese Revolutionary Army). The defection of forces loyal to former CNDP leaders Bosco Ntaganda and Sultani Makenga led the SSF to shift its focus and forces to North and South Kivu, where the M23 operated, creating a security vacuum in areas from which FARDC elements withdrew. The UN Group of Experts on the DRC (UNGOE), HRW, and other observers reported that M23 received a wide range of support from the Rwandan government and, to a lesser extent, from individuals in Uganda.

Foreign RMG, including Forces Democratiques de Liberation du Rwanda (FDLR) and the LRA, indigenous RMG that were supported by foreign governments such as the M23, and some Mai-Mai (local militia) groups increasingly formed loose coalitions during the year and continued to battle government forces and each other and to attack civilian populations. Alliances frequently changed between local militias in apparent attempts to profit from a dynamic situation. Many Mai Mai groups took advantage of the SSF focus on the M23 and the resulting security vacuum. Consequently, a sharp increase occurred in the number of human rights violations in both North Kivu and South Kivu, committed in particular by the M23 in Rutshuru Territory, Mai Mai Lumumba in Lubero Territory, and Raia Mutomboki and Nyatura in South Kivu and North Kivu. The intensified fighting in the East, which impeded humanitarian aid in some areas, increased the number of displaced persons to more than 2.4 million by year's end, exacerbating an already severe humanitarian crisis.

MONUSCO continued to assist the government in seeking to establish and maintain peace and security, particularly in the East. In June the UN Security Council extended MONUSCO's mandate for 12 months and reiterated its mandate to protect civilians. At year's end MONUSCO was comprised of approximately 19,000 peacekeepers, military observers, and police.

Killings: According to reports by UN agencies and NGOs, SSF summarily executed or otherwise killed civilians. Impunity remained a significant problem, and several senior SSF officers continued to hold their positions despite credible evidence of their direct involvement in serious human rights abuses or failure to hold subordinates accountable for such abuses (see section 1.d.).

Abductions: UN agencies and NGOs reported that RMG and some SSF abducted individuals. Generally, individuals were abducted to serve as porters, guides, or in some other capacity.

For additional information see the Department of State's annual *Trafficking in Persons Report* at www.state.

Physical Abuse, Punishment, and Torture: UN agencies and NGOs also reported that SSF arrested, illegally detained, raped, and tortured civilians. The most common offense, by the FARDC in particular, was the looting of villages during military actions against RMG.

There were credible reports from the UNJHRO and other human rights organizations that between November 20 and November 30, 2012 SSF committed multiple killings, rape and plunder in and around the town of Minova, North Kivu.

At least 126 women and girls were reported raped in the incident. Two soldiers were arrested in November in connection with the rapes in Minova. At year's end the government's investigation was ongoing.

RMG committed numerous serious abuses, especially in rural areas of North Kivu, South Kivu, and Orientale, killing, raping, and torturing civilians. Increasingly during the year, RMG forcibly recruited individuals, including children, to serve as porters, guides, and combatants. In certain areas in the East, RMG looted, extorted, and illegally taxed and detained civilians, often for ransom.

For example, on June 24 and 25, nearly 100 fighters suspected of belonging to Mai Mai Lumumba twice attacked the Okapi Wildlife Reserve in Mambasa Territory. At least six civilians and six wardens were killed, and at least 51 women were raped. The attackers also looted the village. More than 100 individuals were abducted to be porters, and 22 women were used as sex slaves. Seventeen of these 22 were presumed to be in the perpetrators' custody at year's end. The military prosecutor opened an investigation and issued an arrest warrant for "Morgan," the reported leader of the Mai Mai Lumumba group.

No progress was made in the trial of the seven surviving individuals accused of organizing the 2010 Walikale mass rapes. In July and August 2010, a coalition of the FDLR, Mai-Mai Cheka, Patriotic Forces for the Liberation of Congo, and combatants led by Colonel Emmanuel Nsengiyumva, a former member of the CNDP and FARDC, allegedly raped 303 women, children, and men in 13 villages in Walikale, North Kivu. The perpetrators also looted more than 1,000 homes and abducted 116 civilians, whom they subjected to forced labor. According to the UN, one of the villages attacked, Luvungi, where more than 100 persons were raped, was a lucrative target because it was a mining hub located only four miles from gold mines. One arrested individual escaped Goma's central prison when the city was overtaken by M23 on November 20. All seven accused in the case remained at large. By year's end no date had been set for the trial to reconvene.

During the year men, women, and minors were raped as part of the violence among RMG and between RMG and the FARDC. Statistics for rape, especially rape of males, were difficult to compile. Heal Africa, an NGO headquartered in Goma, recorded 178 male and 2,339 female survivors of sexual violence, including 745 minors, in 14 clinics in North Kivu in the first six months of the year.

Child Soldiers: The recruitment and use of children in North Kivu, South Kivu, and Orientale provinces by RMG and the FARDC continued (particularly within the poorly integrated elements, including ex-CNDP). The government took steps to reduce and limit the use of child soldiers, including by signing and initiating the implementation of a UN-backed Action Plan to end the recruitment and use of child soldiers, starting awareness campaigns for FARDC personnel, and working with partner organizations to ensure children were not recruited by the FARDC and to develop training materials. In addition FARDC commanders made an increased effort to remove child soldiers, particularly when FARDC elements retook command of units that had been led by ex-CNDP commanders. In multiple instances incoming FARDC commanders requested assistance from MONUSCO, UNICEF, or other humanitarian organizations and transferred children to their care.

Also see the Department of State's annual *Trafficking in Persons Report* at www.state.

Other Conflict-related Abuses: Fighting between the FARDC and RMG continued to displace populations and limit humanitarian access to conflict areas, particularly in the eastern part of the country. According to the UN Office for the Coordination of Humanitarian Affairs (OCHA), there were 215 security incidents against humanitarian agency personnel during the year. All but 18 of those were in North and South Kivu. (From January to September 2011, there were 116 security incidents against humanitarian workers.)

In North Kivu and South Kivu, RMG and elements of the FARDC continued to illegally exploit and trade natural resources for revenue and power. Clandestine trade in minerals and other natural resources facilitated the purchase of weapons and reduced government revenues. The natural resources most exploited were the minerals cassiterite (tin ore), coltan (tantalum ore), wolframite (tungsten ore), and gold, followed by timber, charcoal, and fish. According to media and other reports, the LRA began trafficking in ivory from elephants in Garamba National Park to finance its operations.

The illegal trade in minerals continued to be both a symptom and a cause of the conflict in the Kivu provinces. However, due to enhanced government regulation of the mining and trade of cassiterite and coltan, little legal exportation from North Kivu and South Kivu took place during the year. RMG continue to control and threaten remote mining areas in North Kivu and South Kivu. The M23 imposed illegal taxation on vehicular trade in parts of North Kivu, ensuring profits from smugglers.

The law prohibits the FARDC and RMG from engaging in the mineral trade. However, the government did not effectively enforce the law. Criminal involvement by FARDC units and RMG included protection rackets (such as protection fees paid by mining pit managers to avoid pillage or to facilitate smuggling), indirect commercial control (including the use of illegal "tax" revenues to buy and sell minerals near mining sites), and direct coercive control (including pillage). In addition FARDC units and RMG routinely extorted illegal taxes from civilians and at times forced civilians to work for them or relinquish their mineral production.

The UNGOE reported that several RMG and units of SSF profited from illegal trade and exploitation in the mineral sector and that smuggling of minerals through Rwanda and Burundi increased. In July the government authorized all export houses, including TTT/CMM and Huaying Trading

Company (which it had ordered closed in 2011), to export their "stock" minerals that originated in Maniema Province, which it deemed conflict-free. The UNGOE reported that exports resumed and that both TTT/CMM and Huaying used this "stock" provision to mix and insert minerals of indeterminate origin into their stock exports.

There were credible reports that the following armed groups perpetrated serious human rights abuses in DRC during the year: Alliance des Patriots pour un Congo Libre et Souverain (APCLS), ADF/NALU, Coalition of Ituri Armed Groups, FDLR, Forces Nationales de Liberation, Forces de la Defense Congolaise (FDC- Luanda), Forces de Resistance Patriotique d'Ituri, LRA, M23 (aka Congolese Revolutionary Army), Nyatura, Patriotes Resistants Congolaise, Raia Mutomboki, and the following Mai Mai groups: Cheka, Gedeon, Kifuafua, Lumumba, Morgan/Simba/Manu/Luc, Pareco, Shetani, and Yakutumba.

SECTION 2. RESPECT FOR CIVIL LIBERTIES, INCLUDING

a. Freedom of Speech and Press

The law provides for freedom of speech and press. In practice the government rarely infringed on individuals' freedom of speech unless exercised in the media. According to media-focused NGOs, freedom of the press declined during the year. Generally, individuals could privately criticize the government, its officials, and other private citizens without being subject to official reprisals. However, certain regulating bodies intimidated journalists and publishers into practicing self- censorship. Public criticism of government officials and government conduct or decisions regarding issues such as conflict and insurgencies, management of natural resources, and corruption sometimes resulted in harsh responses, often from the ANR, and, less frequently, from provincial authorities.

Freedom of Speech: While the law provides for freedom of speech, it potentially inhibits this freedom through its prohibition on insulting the head of state. In addition the 2004 penal code criminalizes malicious and public slander. In practice these laws were not enforced, and the government regularly respected its citizens' freedom of speech, provided that it was not exercised in the media.

The Conseil Superieur de l'Audiovisuel et de la Communication (CSAC) is mandated to guarantee freedom and protection of the press and to ensure equal access for political parties, associations, and citizens to official means of communication and information. In practice, CSAC lacked the capacity to monitor adequately all of the media outlets operating across the country, and media, human rights, and other organizations regularly questioned its power, independence, and neutrality. In addition legal ambiguities created conflict between the CSAC and the Ministry of Media, which according to the 1996 law on the press has the power to suspend media activities. CSAC's founding legislation, and the powers it outlines for the regulatory body, were presumed to supplant this 1996 law, but it has never been amended.

A large and active private press (both pro- and antigovernment) functioned throughout the country, and the government licensed a large number of daily newspapers. According to the Ministry of Communications, 134 television stations, 463 radio stations, and 445 newspapers were registered as of August. The government required newspapers to pay a one-time license fee of 250,000 Congolese francs (approximately $270) and complete several administrative requirements before publishing. Many journalists lacked professional training, received little or no set salary, and were willing to work for wealthy individuals, government officials, and politicians who paid for specific articles.

Radio remained the most important medium of public information due to limited literacy and the relatively high cost of newspapers and television. The state owned three radio stations and three television stations, and the president's family owned two television stations. The majority of media outlets were owned or operated by government officials and politicians.

In 2010 government authorities added a provision in journalists' letters of accreditation that the military code of justice (concerning criminal penalties, including imprisonment) applied to any foreign journalists who committed press offenses. In response international journalists expressed concern over their ability to report on sensitive subjects such as the conflict in the East and corruption. At year's end there were no known cases in which this policy was applied.

Violence and Harassment: On June 14, CSAC issued a directive urging journalists to report responsibly on the conflict in the East and to commit to promoting national unity as they carry out their duties. The directive warned that media organizations whose reports might be construed as attempts to demoralize the military or the population could face charges of treason. While the order was primarily directed at deterring hate speech and ethnic attacks (which are illegal under both the 1996 law on the press and the 2011 law that established the CSAC), many in the media community perceived it as an indirect way to undermine the independent media's ability to report freely on conflict-related developments. Its impact was felt by the most popular radio station across the country, Radio Okapi, an independent radio station jointly founded by MONUSCO and the Foundation Hirondelle with support from various international donors. Okapi's journalists and staff received multiple threats from unidentified sources, and CSAC cut its signal on December 1. While CSAC reported the signal was cut because Okapi had not submitted necessary paperwork, others argued that CSAC acted after Okapi broadcast an interview with M23's political leader. Radio Okapi's signal was restored on December 4.

SSF beat, arbitrarily arrested, harassed, and intimidated local journalists because of their reporting. According to Journaliste en danger (JED), six journalists were beaten and 23 were threatened or harassed during the year. For example, JED reported that Franck Zongwe, a cameraman with Vision Shala TV, was beaten by national police officers after photographing an accident involving the police. Zongwe later recovered his camera, which the police chief had confiscated.

In addition JED reported an increase (from 160 in 2011 to 175 in 2012) in attacks on press freedom. These attacks included journalists who were detained, questioned, attacked, mistreated, tortured, threatened or harassed, or subjected to administrative, judicial, or economic pressure, as well as obstacles to the free circulation of information. Notably, no journalists were killed or disappeared during the year. However, there were increases in journalists questioned (46 in 2012 compared with 22 in 2011) and restrictions on free circulation of information (75 in 2012 versus 43 in 2011). Also noteworthy, there were 22 fewer incidents of journalists being attacked, mistreated, or tortured (six cases in 2012 and 28 cases in 2011).

Censorship or Content Restrictions: While CSAC is, by law, the only institution with the authority to restrict broadcasts, the government, including SSF and provincial officials, also exercised this power in practice. For example, on July 12, the minister of media suspended the director of the national media outlet, Radio Television Nationale Congolaise (RTNC), for allowing it to broadcast a meeting of the pro-Kabila People's Party for Reconstruction and Democracy (PPRD) that was purportedly characterized by "xenophobic rhetoric." According to the government, some PPRD members made statements that "undermine national unity and come under the law that condemns incitement to ethnic and tribal hatred." In addition, on December 31, 2011, authorities suspended Radio France Internationale's broadcasts for having broadcast opposition leader Etienne Tshisekedi's New Year's national address alongside that of President Kabila. According to the information minister, giving Tshisekedi's speech a status equivalent to the president's supported Tshisekedi's "anticonstitutional comedy."

The Media Ministry shut down pro-opposition Canal Futur TV and Radio Television Lisanga for reasons not made clear. The ministry variously cited administrative or security reasons as the rationale for these closures, but according to media watchdogs, it failed to present credible evidence to support its claims.

Libel Laws/National Security: The national and provincial governments continued to use criminal defamation and insult laws to intimidate and punish those critical of the government. For example, on April 15, the PNC detained Sebastien Mulumba and Mbuyi Mukadi of *Kisangani News* after they published an unfavorable article about a national deputy. In addition the government did not permit the broadcasting of the documentary film by Thierry Michel, *The Chebeya Affair, a Crime of the State?* (L'affaire Chebeya, un crime d'Etat?) According to the Federation Internationale des Ligues des Droits de l'Homme and the Organisation Mondiale Contre la Torture, former minister of justice and human rights Luzolo recommended that the film be suppressed because he believed it contained false allegations against the president.

Nongovernmental Impact: RMG and their political wings regularly restricted the press and journalists operating in the areas in which they operated. For example, JED reported that on November 20, three Kinshasa-based stations, RTNC, Digital Congo, and Radio Television du Groupe l'Avenir had their Goma-based relay stations cut and transferred to M23 control. In addition M23 elements and leaders threatened various journalists, including Jean-Baptiste Kambale, the director of Community Radio Ushirika, in Rutshuru on September 25 and again on October 15 after he broadcast a report on TV5 Monde on the M23 rebels and their attacks on the civilian population.

Internet Freedom

The government did not restrict access to the Internet or monitor e-mail or Internet chat rooms. The CSAC law stipulates that bloggers must obtain authorization from CSAC. At year's end CSAC had not refused authorization to any bloggers. Private entrepreneurs made Internet access available at moderate prices through Internet cafes in large cities throughout the country. According to the International Telecommunication Union, 1.2 percent of individuals used the Internet in 2011.

Academic Freedom and Cultural Events

There were no government restrictions on academic freedom or cultural events.

b. Freedom of Peaceful Assembly and Association

Freedom of Assembly

The constitution provides for freedom of peaceful assembly. The government sometimes restricted this right.

The government requires organizers of public events to register with local authorities in advance. To deny authorization, authorities must do so in writing within five days of registration. State security forces occasionally acted against unregistered protests, marches, or meetings.

On occasion authorities denied permission to hold demonstrations, in particular to opposition parties and their civil society allies. For example, according to some observers, on February 16, SSF used force and tear gas to disperse participants in a march organized by the Council of Catholic Laymen in the Congo to commemorate the 20th anniversary of the Limete Catholic massacre by presidential guards. The day before the march, authorities announced that the march was prohibited due to the organizers' failure to notify them of their plans. A limited number of people marched anyway and were met with a significant police presence. Three individuals were arrested, but no injuries were reported.

The government continued to investigate violence around elections, including a November 2011 incident in which HRW reported that 12 opposition supporters and bystanders were killed and 41 individuals injured when rival supporters gathered to greet both Etienne Tshisekedi and President Kabila at Kinshasa's N'djili Airport.

Freedom of Association

The constitution provides for freedom of association. In practice the government generally respected this right.

c. Freedom of Religion

See the Department of State's *International Religious Freedom Report* at www.state.

d. Freedom of Movement, Internally Displaced Persons, Protection of Refugees, and Stateless Persons

The law provides for freedom of internal movement, foreign travel, emigration, and repatriation. The government sometimes restricted these rights.

In-country Movement: SSF--and to a greater extent RMG--established barriers and checkpoints on roads and at ports, airports, and markets, ostensibly for security reasons, and routinely harassed and extorted money from civilians for supposed violations, sometimes detaining them until they or a relative paid. The government required travelers to submit to immigration procedures during domestic travel at airports, ports, and when entering and leaving towns.

Local authorities continued to collect illegal taxes and fees from boats traveling on many parts of the Congo River. There were also widespread reports of FARDC soldiers and RMG extorting fees from persons taking goods to market or traveling between towns (see section 1.g.).

SSF sometimes required travelers to present official travel orders from an employer or government official, although the law does not require such documentation. SSF often detained individuals traveling without official orders in order to pressure bribes.

Foreign Travel: As a result of inadequate administrative systems, passport issuance was often irregular. Officials regularly accepted bribes to expedite the application process.

Internally Displaced Persons (IDPs)

Due to heightened conflict in the East, the number of IDPs increased to more than 2.4 million throughout the country, according to the Office of the UN High Commissioner for Refugees (UNHCR). On December 11, OCHA reported that more than 900,000 people were displaced in North Kivu. Of those, 500,000 were displaced following the start of the M23 armed conflict in

April. Displacement also remained a problem in South Kivu, Orientale, Equateur, Katanga, and Maniema provinces. The conflict in the East and the actions of numerous RMG profiting from the increased insecurity were considered the primary causes of displacement.

The government was not able to adequately protect or assist IDPs, who were forced to rely heavily on humanitarian organizations. The government generally allowed domestic and international humanitarian organizations to provide assistance to IDPs. However, fighting by RMG and a general lack of security impeded their efforts.

As of November 30, approximately 105,000 IDPs lived in 31 sites and camps managed by international NGOs and coordinated by the UNHCR. Those residing outside camps stayed with host families, friends or relatives, found shelter in schools or other buildings, or found refuge in the forest.

Some IDPs in North Kivu were victims of abuses, including sexual exploitation of women and children, abduction, forced conscription, looting, plundering of crops, illegal taxation, and general harassment, by all factions engaged in fighting and by other civilians. For example, the UNHCR reported more than 7,000 protection incidents between April and July 15, noting that most of the victims were villagers and IDPs. Displaced women and children were vulnerable to abuses, including rape and forced recruitment, by the FARDC, RMG, and civilians.

Protection of Refugees

As of November there were 137,164 refugees in the country from seven adjacent countries, the majority from Angola and Rwanda. In addition there were 441,598 Congolese refugees recorded as residing in other African countries, the majority of whom were in Uganda, the Republic of the Congo, Tanzania, Rwanda, and Burundi.

Access to Asylum: The law provides for the granting of asylum or refugee status, and the government has established a rudimentary system for providing protection to refugees. In practice it granted refugee and asylum status and provided protection against the expulsion or return of refugees to countries where their lives or freedom would be threatened on account of their race, religion, nationality, membership in a particular social group, or political opinion.

The government provided temporary protection to an undetermined number of individuals who may not qualify as refugees.

The government cooperated with the UNHCR and other humanitarian organizations in assisting refugees and asylum seekers with welfare and safety needs. The government provided assistance in the safe, voluntary return of refugees to their homes by allowing their entry into the country and facilitating their passage through the immigration system. In establishing security mechanisms, government authorities did not treat refugees differently than citizens.

Through the application of the cessation clauses of the 1951 Convention and the 1969 Organization of African Unity Convention, Angolans ceased to be refugees on June 30. Between November 2011 and that date, 17,111 refugees returned voluntarily to Angola. An additional 70,000 former Angolan refugees remained in the country, 22,000 of whom indicated a desire to return to Angola and 48,000 of whom expressed a desire to integrate locally in the DRC. The government agreed to issue temporary residence permits at a significantly reduced cost to former refugees wishing to integrate locally.

As of November 30, 10,379 refugees had returned voluntarily to Rwanda and 480 refugees had returned voluntarily to Burundi.

SECTION 3. RESPECT FOR POLITICAL RIGHTS: THE RIGHT OF CITIZENS TO CHANGE THEIR GOVERNMENT

The constitution provides citizens the right to change their government peacefully, and in 2011 citizens exercised this right through presidential and parliamentary elections based on universal suffrage.

Elections and Political Participation

Recent Elections: Presidential and parliamentary elections were held in November 2011, and Joseph Kabila was declared president in December. Several international observer missions judged that the results of the elections "lacked credibility," due largely to irregularities and a lack of transparency in the vote tabulation process.

On January 27, after multiple delays, the National Independent Electoral Commission (CENI) announced partial results for the parliamentary elections. The CENI released complete provisional results on February 2, announcing

483 provisional winners and referring the remaining 17 seats to the Supreme Court for adjudication and possible annulment due to significant irregularities. By early February the Supreme Court had approximately 5,000 cases to consider, in which approximately 340 seats were contested. Many of these cases reportedly had little merit, were presented without documentation and with no legal counsel, and were dismissed on procedural grounds. On April 27, the Supreme Court finalized its review, certified the results of 482 electoral contests and invalidated 32 of the CENI's provisional results. The court also ordered that the CENI release the names of 10 winners of remote districts in the center of the country and that new elections be held for seven seats representing North Kivu's Masisi Territory and one seat representing Equateur's Befale District. The CENI released the names of the winners of the 10 remote districts on June 19. On September 20, after giving the CENI two extensions to comply with its directive to rerun the elections, the Supreme Court ordered the CENI to publish the names of those who had nominally won the seats on November 28, 2011. At year's end the Befale elections had not been conducted.

From February 16 to 29, the National Assembly held its extraordinary session in which the secretary general validated the mandates of the elected officials. A number of members of the UDPS party, the main opposition party, chose not to attend to protest the outcome of the election and to support the claim made by Union for Democracy and Social Progress (UDPS) leader Etienne Tshisekedi that he had been legitimately elected president.

On April 18, President Kabila named Augustin Matata Ponyo as prime minister. Matata named his cabinet on April 28.

On April 19, the CENI completed its review of its performance during the national election.

By year's end a date for provincial and local elections, originally scheduled for early 2012, had not been rescheduled.

Political Parties: The 2007 law on the status and rights of the political opposition recognizes opposition parties represented in parliament as well as those not in parliament. The law also details the various "sacred" rights and obligations of opposition parties. Although political parties were able to operate most of the time without restriction or outside interference, opposition members were sometimes harassed. For example, UDPS secretary general Jacquemain Shabani was arrested at N'djili aiport on February 7 when trying to depart the country. He alleged he was mistreated by ANR, while authorities claimed he was carrying "incriminating documents," including leaflets encouraging SSF to disobey authorities and a false passport. He was released one day later.

Participation of Women and Minorities: At year's end women held more than 10 percent of the seats in the National Assembly (49 of 482) and approximately 6 percent in the provincial assemblies (43 of 690). The 2011 elections produced no significant change with respect to female representatives. Six of the 108 senators were women. Among the 37 government ministers and vice ministers, six were women, a significant proportional increase in women in the government formed in 2012 (from 9 percent to 16 percent).

Some ethnic groups, including Pygmies, were not represented in the Senate, the National Assembly, or provincial assemblies. Their lack of political participation may have been a result of the vast ethnic diversity as well as societal discrimination. The enslavement of and discrimination against Pygmies continued in some areas and contributed to their lack of political participation (see section 5).

SECTION 4. CORRUPTION AND LACK OF TRANSPARENCY IN GOVERNMENT

The law provides criminal penalties for official corruption. In 2002 the government established a watchdog agency for the enforcement of the code of professional ethics, which promotes ethical behavior among civil servants in the workplace. The Court of Accounts and the Congolese Anti-Corruption League NGO work closely on corruption matters. In 2007 the government ratified the Southern African Development Community Protocol Against Corruption.

Nevertheless, the authorities did not adequately implement the law, and corruption remained endemic throughout the government and SSF. Bribery was routine in public and private business transactions, especially in the areas of government procurement, dispute settlement, and taxation. The public perceived the government to be widely corrupt at all levels. According to the World Bank's most recent Worldwide Governance Indicators, official corruption was a severe problem.

Corruption in the judicial and penal systems continued to be severe (see section 1.c.). In rural areas where there were often no courts within a 300-mile radius, justice was administered on an ad hoc basis, often by local village authorities with little oversight, creating opportunities for corruption and abuse of power.

Weak financial controls and a poorly functioning judicial system encouraged officials to engage in corruption with impunity. The government began paying many civil servants and security forces in major cities by direct deposit, eliminating an important means of graft. Previously the government utilized a cascading cash payment system in which salaries were dispersed to senior officials for payment to the officials as well as their staffs, continuing downward until all employees were paid. Nevertheless, wages for public employees were inadequate, and officials sought bribes to augment their income.

For those security forces not being paid by direct deposit, embezzlement of soldiers' salaries by FARDC commanders was common and appeared to contribute to extortion, looting, and other abuses by soldiers against citizens (see section 1.d.).

The law criminalizes money laundering and terrorist financing and provides for a Financial Intelligence Unit. However, limited resources and a weak judicial system hampered the government's ability to enforce anti-money laundering regulations. Further, local institutions and personnel lacked the training and capacity to enforce the law and its attendant regulations fully.

Reports, including the UNGOE report, indicated that the mining sector continued to lose millions of dollars because of official corruption at all levels. Additional revenue losses were due to illegal exploitation of minerals in the East by the FARDC (although illegal exploitation by RMG was a more significant problem than exploitation by the FARDC) (see section 1.g.).

The International Monetary Fund (IMF) raised concerns about the nontransparency of mining contracts entered into by the state-owned mining company Gecamines. The IMF and the World Bank noted that Gecamines appeared to be concluding the sale of public assets without adherence to transparency principles. The IMF allowed its Extended Credit Facility program to expire without successful conclusion because the government failed to publish the terms of a controversial mining contract and did not adhere to the New York convention of arbitration.

The Ministry of Justice and Human Rights created an internal anticorruption team in 2011. According to one high level internal source, this structure lacked independence and, therefore, the power to fight corruption.

Government authorities and wealthy individuals at times used antidefamation laws that carry criminal punishments to discourage media investigation of government corruption (see section 2.a.).

The law requires the president and ministers to disclose their assets to a government committee. President Kabila and all ministers and vice ministers reportedly did so during the year. However, the data were not made public.

The law does not provide for public access to government-held information. In practice the government did not grant access either to citizens or noncitizens, including foreign media.

In 2008 the country was accepted as a candidate in the Extractive Industries Transparency Initiative (EITI), an international voluntary initiative designed to increase transparency in transactions between governments and companies in the extractive industries. The government received a final 18-month extension to complete validation by March 1, 2013. On July 13, the EITI executive committee announced that fiscal evasion remained rampant in the extractive industries, a condition that was expected to have an adverse impact on the country's ability to achieve EITI compliance.

SECTION 5. GOVERNMENTAL ATTITUDE REGARDING INTERNATIONAL AND NONGOVERNMENTAL INVESTIGATION OF ALLEGED VIOLATIONS OF HUMAN RIGHTS

While a wide variety of domestic and international human rights organizations investigated and published findings on human rights cases, elements of the SSF continued to harass, beat, intimidate, and arbitrarily arrest and detain domestic human rights advocates and domestic NGO workers. Officials from the Ministry of Justice and Human Rights met with domestic NGOs and sometimes responded to their inquiries.

Domestic human rights NGOs were particularly vulnerable to harassment, arbitrary arrest and detention, and other abuses by SSF when reporting on or supporting victims of abuses by SSF and when spotlighting the illegal exploitation of natural resources in the East. For example, on January 5, the house of a human rights defender was burned under suspicious circumstances after he publicly questioned election irregularities and the government's political will to combat impunity. By year's end no progress had been made on the investigation, and no charges had been filed.

UN and Other International Bodies: The government allowed international humanitarian agencies access to conflict zones, permitted many UN human rights officers to investigate abuses, and invited UN special rapporteurs and representatives to visit the country to assess the human rights situation and provide technical assistance. However, the government did not take meaningful steps to implement their recommendations. There were instances in which authorities obstructed the work of UN human rights monitors and special rapporteurs.

The government generally cooperated with international NGOs that published reports on human rights and humanitarian issues and permitted their investigators access to conflict areas. These human rights and humanitarian aid workers operated in unstable environments where RMG were actively engaged and were sometimes attacked. OCHA documented 123 incidents (almost 60 percent of all incidents) against humanitarian workers during the year in North Kivu.

The government generally cooperated with multilateral organizations. According to the UN, child protection officers were granted increased access to FARDC units, particularly in the East. However, while authorities continued to permit international humanitarian agencies access to conflict areas, authorities denied the agencies access to prisons run by the ANR and the RG located in these areas (see section 1.g.).

The government cooperated with the International Criminal Court (ICC), which, in its first completed trial, convicted Thomas Lubanga Dyilo on March 14 for conscripting, enlisting, and using child soldiers in 2002 and 2003. The ICC again called upon the government to arrest Bosco Ntaganda, who on July 13 became subject to a second arrest warrant for three counts of crimes against humanity, including murder, rape, and persecution, allegedly committed between September 1, 2002, and September 30, 2003, in Ituri, Orientale Province. President Kabila publicly committed on April 11 to arrest Ntaganda and bring him to trial in the DRC, but Ntaganda and several hundred soldiers deserted and launched a mutiny in North Kivu that continued at year's end.

The government continued to cooperate with the International Criminal Tribunal for Rwanda (ICTR), which operated freely in areas under government control, seeking several individuals indicted for involvement in the 1994 Rwandan genocide. In May 2011 Congolese authorities arrested Bernard Munyagishira, allegedly responsible for leading the genocide in the border town of Gisenyi, Rwanda, directly across the border from Goma, North Kivu. On June 7, the ICTR transferred Munyagishira's case to Rwandan authorities. In addition on May 3, Ministry of Justice authorities instructed national

Interpol officials to proceed with the arrest of Ladislas Ntaganzwa, who is subject to an ICTR warrant for, among other crimes, genocide, crimes against humanity, and violations of the Geneva Conventions. Ntaganzwa's case was also transferred to Rwandan authorities on May 9.

Government Human Rights Bodies: On October 10, the National Assembly adopted a law to create a Human Rights Commission. This follows the 2008 adoption of a similar law by the Senate. On December 5, the Senate transferred the harmonized legislation to the Supreme Court for a constitutionality review. Although the government organized an Interministerial Human Rights Committee, which meets on an ad hoc basis to address high-profile issues, its effectiveness remained limited.

SECTION 6. DISCRIMINATION, SOCIETAL ABUSES, AND TRAFFICKING IN PERSONS

The constitution prohibits discrimination based on ethnicity, gender, or religion. The government did not enforce these prohibitions effectively.

In many cases throughout this section data from prior years are presented because more recent data were not available. In all such cases observers believed that the situation had not materially improved during the year.

Women

Rape and Domestic Violence: The law criminalizes rape, but the government did not effectively enforce this law, and rape was common throughout the country. The law defines rape to include male victims, sexual slavery, sexual harassment, forced pregnancy, and other sexual crimes, but not spousal rape. It also prohibits compromise fines and forced marriage, allows victims of sexual violence to waive appearance in court, and permits closed hearings to protect confidentiality. The minimum penalty prescribed for rape is a prison sentence of five years.

SSF, RMG, and civilians perpetrated widespread and sometimes mass rape of women and girls (see section 1.g.). Between December 2010 and November 2011, the UN reported a total of 625 cases of sexual violence perpetrated by parties to the conflict in North Kivu, South Kivu, and Orientale provinces. Of these, 602 were against women and girls and 23 were against men and boys. The UN reported that almost half of the incidents were attributed to the FARDC and the PNC, noting that this high proportion could be explained by the greater access human rights monitors had to areas under SSF control. Separately, the Ministry of Gender reported 11,672 cases of sexual- and gender-based violence in 2011 in North Kivu, South Kivu, Ituri district, Bandundu, Bas-Congo, Katanga, and Kinshasa. Of these cases, 10,037 were reported in North Kivu, South Kivu, and Ituri.

Statistical information on rape remained fragmented and incomplete. Statistics often came from international and local NGO service providers and therefore were skewed towards priority implementation areas. For example, the Ministry of Gender was unable to supply information for Equateur, Kasai Occidental, Kasai Oriental, and Maniema provinces.

Prosecutions for rape and other types of sexual violence remained rare, although there were indications that the situation had improved. The UN reported that through its support, military justice prosecuted 355 cases of serious human rights violations from July 2010 to June 2011, an increase from 337 during the previous 12 months. UN sources attributed this increase to the rise in prosecutions for sexual violence crimes and noted that this trend continued throughout the year. Nevertheless, both victims and the UN Human Rights Council's (UNHRC) special rapporteur on violence against women cited widespread impunity as the main reason for sexual violence. Most victims did not have sufficient confidence in the justice system to pursue formal legal action or feared subjecting themselves to further humiliation and possible reprisal.

It was common for family members to pressure a rape victim to remain silent, even with health care professionals, to safeguard the reputations of the victim and her family. Victims of SGBV faced enormous social stigma. After a sexual assault, many young women and girls were labeled as unsuitable for marriage, and married women were frequently abandoned by their husbands. Some families forced rape victims to marry the men who raped them or to forego prosecution in exchange for money or goods from the rapist.

Domestic violence was common throughout the country. For example, according to the 2007 Demographic Health Survey (DHS), 71 percent of women reported some form of sexual, mental, or physical abuse. Other sources found that 86 percent of women in Equateur Province were victims of domestic abuse. While there were few recent statistics available regarding the extent of domestic abuse, a Kinshasa-based December 2010 survey of 1,000 individuals conducted by Les Experts found that 45 percent of respondents had been abused. Although the law considers assault a crime, it does not specifically address spousal abuse, and police rarely intervened in domestic disputes. There were no reports of judicial authorities taking action in cases of domestic or spousal abuse.

Female Genital Mutilation/Cutting (FGM/C): The law prohibits FGM/C. Current data on the prevalence of FGM/C did not exist.

Sexual Harassment: Sexual harassment occurred throughout the country. A 2010 study conducted by the World Health Organization found that 64 percent of all workers surveyed had experienced sexual harassment at the workplace. The law prohibits sexual harassment, and the minimum penalty prescribed by law is a prison sentence of one year. There was little or no effective enforcement.

Reproductive Rights: The government respected the right of couples to decide freely and responsibly the number, spacing, and timing of their children and to have the information and means to do so free from discrimination, coercion, and violence. However, while the law does not require spousal permission for family planning usage, it was common practice for providers to require a husband's permission before providing family planning services. Women's access to contraception remained extremely low. Only 5.8 percent of women used modern contraceptive methods and, according to the 2010 Multiple Indicator Cluster Survey, total unmet need for family planning was almost 24 percent. According to UN estimates, the maternal mortality rate for 2010 was 540 deaths per 100,000 live births, and a woman's lifetime risk of maternal death was 1 in 30.

The extent of women's access to treatment for sexually transmitted diseases was not known. Recent studies did not disaggregate by gender, and the data were highly variable across geographic regions, reflecting variations in cultural norms and access to health-care services. The percentage of women seeking skilled medical assistance during childbirth was 74 percent, according to the 2007 DHS.

According to the 2010 Cluster Survey conducted by the government with various UN agencies and a foreign aid agency, 87 percent of pregnant women received prenatal care at least once from a qualified professional. This represented a 2 percent increase from the 2007 DHS. Medical assistance during childbirth was not as prevalent as prenatal care, but access increased between 2001 and 2007. Education, socioeconomic status, place of delivery (hospital, clinic, or home), and geographic location had a significant impact on who received postpartum care. While societal and cultural norms suggest women (and their husbands) prefer large families and therefore do not use family planning methods, there were no cultural barriers to seeking health care except for a minority who belonged to Bunda dia Mayala (formerly known as Bunda dia Congo), a political and religious movement in which adherents are not vaccinated.

Discrimination: Women did not possess the same rights as men in some respects, both under the law and in practice. The law requires a married woman to obtain her husband's consent before engaging in legal transactions, including selling or renting real estate, opening a bank account, or applying for a passport. According to UNICEF, many widows were dispossessed of their property. Women found guilty of adultery may be sentenced to up to one year in prison, while adultery by men is punishable only if judged to have "an injurious quality."

In their 2009 report to the UNHRC, seven UN special rapporteurs and representatives expressed concern that, while the family code recognizes equality between spouses, it "effectively renders a married woman a minor under the guardianship of her husband" by stating that the wife must obey her husband.

Women experienced economic discrimination. The law forbids a woman from working at night or accepting employment without her husband's consent. According to the International Labor Organization, women often received less pay in the private sector than men doing the same job and rarely occupied positions of authority or high responsibility.

The constitution calls for gender parity. Various laws require political parties to consider gender when presenting candidates at all levels. However, only approximately 12 percent of the candidates in the 2011 legislative elections were women.

Children

Birth Registration: According to UNICEF, 50.6 percent of children whose births were observed in some form of medical facility were registered with the state. Birth registration was lowest among ethnic minorities such as Pygmies. The lack of registration did not affect access to government services.

Education: The constitution and law stipulate that public primary education shall be free and compulsory until 16 years of age. In practice, however, primary school education was not compulsory, tuition-free, or universal, and few functioning government-funded schools existed. Public and private schools generally expected parents to contribute to teachers' salaries, and parents typically funded 80 to 90 percent of school expenses. These expenses, combined with the potential loss of income or labor while their children attended class, rendered many parents unable or unwilling to enroll their children. In 2009 President Kabila ordered the gradual implementation of a fee-free policy for primary schools in all areas except the cities of Kinshasa and Lubumbashi. However, the executive order was not effectively implemented, and the inadequate education budget severely limited the state's ability to implement its free primary education policy. As a result most schools continued to rely on fees paid by parents.

Primary and secondary school attendance rates for girls were lower than for boys due to financial, cultural, and/or security reasons. The World Bank reported in July that 72 percent of females between the ages of 15 and 24 attended school, while 78 percent of males in the same age range attended.

Many of the schools in conflict zones were dilapidated and had been closed due to insecurity. Others were used as housing for IDPs. The FDLR and Mai Mai groups, as well as some FARDC units, were responsible for several lootings and occupations of schools. According to UNICEF, at least 240,000 children missed schooling as a result of the M23 conflict. On December 10, UNICEF also reported that approximately 600 schools had been looted or damaged in North and South Kivu since April. Parents in some areas prohibited their children from attending schools due to fear that RMG would forcibly recruit them.

Child Abuse: Although the law prohibits all forms of child abuse, it regularly occurred. There was no information about authorities arresting individuals for child abandonment or other abuse.

The constitution prohibits parental abandonment of children who are believed to have committed sorcery. Nevertheless, parents or other care providers sometimes abandoned or abused such children, frequently invoking "witchcraft" as a rationale, regardless of whether or not they believed their child was a "witch." The law provides for a sentence of imprisonment for parents and other adults who accuse children of witchcraft. Authorities did not implement the law effectively.

Many churches conducted exorcisms of children accused of witchcraft involving isolation, beating and whipping, starvation, and forced ingestion of purgatives. According to UNICEF, children with disabilities or speech impediments were sometimes branded as witches. This practice sometimes resulted in parents abandoning their children. In addition UNICEF stated that as many as 70 percent of the street children it assisted claimed to have been accused of witchcraft.

In 2009 a group of seven UN special rapporteurs and representatives mandated by the UNHRC to assess human rights in the country deemed it "alarming" that a significant percentage of the victims of sexual violence were girls and in some cases boys. The Ministry of Gender reported that of 4,464 survivors of SGBV reporting their age in 2011, 1,214 were between the ages of 10 and 17, and 249 were younger than 10. Of the overall number, 33 percent were children.

Several NGOs, including Save the Children, worked with MONUSCO and UNICEF to promote children's rights throughout the country.

Child Marriage: While the law prohibits marriage of girls under the age of 14 and boys younger than 18, some marriages of underage girls took place. Dowry payments greatly contributed to underage marriage, as parents married off a daughter against her will to collect a dowry or to finance a dowry for a son.

The law criminalizes forced marriage. It subjects parents to up to 12 years' hard labor and a fine of 92,500 Congolese francs ($100) for forcing a child to marry. The penalty doubles when the child is under the age of 15. There were no reports of prosecutions for forced marriage.

Sexual Exploitation of Children: The minimum age of consensual sex is 14 for females and 18 for males, and the law prohibits prostitution by anyone under the age of 18. Nevertheless, child prostitution occurred throughout the country, although there were no statistics available regarding its prevalence. Some of these children engaged in prostitution without third-party involvement, while others were forced to do so.

According to a 2010 World Bank report, 26 percent of children living on the streets were girls, and of these, nine of 10 were involved in prostitution, and seven of 10 had been raped. The NGO Heal Africa reported that sexual abuse of children is more prevalent in rural areas.

Child Soldiers: Many parties to the conflict in the East used child soldiers. The M23 was particularly notorious for recruiting child combatants (see section 1.g.).

Displaced Children: According to the 2007 DHS, there were an estimated 8.2 million orphans and vulnerable children in the country. Ninety-one percent received no external support of any kind, and only 3 percent received medical support. In 2006 UNICEF and the World Bank estimated that 30,000-40,000 children lived on the streets, with the highest concentration in Kinshasa. Many of these children were forced out of their homes when their families accused them of witchcraft and bringing misfortune to their families. Others were child refugees and war orphans. The situation was not believed to have improved materially since these reports.

The government was ill equipped to deal with such large numbers of homeless children. SSF abused and arbitrarily arrested street children (see sections 1.c. and 1.d.).

International Child Abductions: The country is not a party to the 1980 Hague Convention on the Civil Aspects of International Child Abduction.

Anti-Semitism

The country has a very small Jewish population, and there were no reports of anti- Semitic acts.

Trafficking in Persons

See the Department of State's *Trafficking in Persons Report* at www.state.

Persons with Disabilities

The 2006 constitution prohibits discrimination against persons with disabilities, stipulates that all citizens regardless of their abilities have access to public services, including education, and provides that persons with disabilities are afforded specific protections by the government. In addition the labor code states that private, public, and semipublic companies cannot discriminate against qualified candidates based on their intellectual, sensorial, and physical disabilities. The government did not effectively enforce these provisions, and persons with disabilities often found it difficult to obtain employment, education, or government services.

The law does not mandate access to buildings or government services for persons with disabilities. Some schools for persons with disabilities, including persons with visual disabilities, received private funds and limited public funds to provide education and vocational training. The Ministry of Social Affairs, together with other applicable ministries (Labor, Education, Justice, Health), has the lead in ensuring persons with disabilities are treated equally.

According to UNICEF, children with disabilities or speech impediments were sometimes branded as witches.

National/Racial/Ethnic Minorities

Members of the country's more than 400 ethnic groups practiced ethnic discrimination, and discrimination was evident in hiring patterns in some cities. The government took no reported actions to address this problem.

Indigenous People

The country had a population of between 200,000 and 500,000 Pygmies (Twa, Mbuti, Aka, and others), believed to be the country's original inhabitants. Societal discrimination against them was widespread, and the government did not effectively protect their civil and political rights. Most Pygmies took no part in the political process and lived in remote areas. Fighting in the East between RMG and SSF caused displacement of some

Pygmy populations. Since 2003 many Pygmies who had lived in IDP camps in the East were forced out of the camps by other IDPs, removing their access to humanitarian relief provided to camp residents.

In some areas Pygmies were kidnapped and forced into slavery.

Societal Abuses, Discrimination, and Acts of Violence Based on Sexual Orientation and Gender Identity

While there are no laws specifically prohibiting homosexuality or homosexual acts, individuals engaging in public displays of homosexuality were subject to prosecution under public decency provisions in the penal code and articles in the law on sexual violence. Homosexuality remained a cultural taboo, and harassment by SSF was believed to have continued. The Ministry of Health actively worked with LGBT groups in a nondiscriminatory fashion to reduce the stigma and prevent new HIV infections among men who have sex with men.

Other Societal Violence or Discrimination

There were no reports of societal violence or discrimination based on HIV/AIDS status.

Discrimination against persons with albinism was widespread and limited their ability to obtain employment, health care, and education and to marry. Persons with albinism were frequently ostracized by their families and communities.

SECTION 7. WORKER RIGHTS

a. Freedom of Association and the Right to Collective Bargaining

The constitution and the 2002 labor code provide all workers, except government officials and members of SSF, the right to form and join trade unions without prior authorization or excessive requirements, to conduct legal strikes, and to bargain collectively. Additionally, the law provides unions the right to conduct activities without interference. However, the provision does not clearly define specific acts of interference. In the private sector a minimum of 10 employees are required for unionizing a business, and more than one union can be represented within a single business. Collective bargaining requires a minimum of 10 union committee members plus one employer representative. Union committee members report to the rest of the workforce. Foreigners cannot hold union office unless they have lived in the country for at least 20 years. The union committee is required to notify the company's management of a planned strike; it does not need authorization to strike. However, the law stipulates that unions and employers shall adhere to lengthy mandatory arbitration and appeal procedures before unions initiate a strike. In general the committee delivers a notice to strike to the employer and then waits for a reply for 48 hours. The employer is not obligated to reply. If it chooses to reply, negotiations, which may take up to three months, begin with a labor inspector and ultimately, the Peace Court. If the employer does not reply within 48 hours, the union may strike immediately. Sometimes employees provide only minimum labor while negotiating.

The police, army, and domestic workers cannot strike. Directors in public and private enterprises are also excluded from striking. Unless employers are notified of a planned strike, workers are not allowed to occupy the workplace during a strike, and an infraction of the rules on strikes may lead to incarceration of up to six months. However, if unions notify their employer of a strike, the workers can occupy the workplace without violating the labor code.

The law prohibits discrimination against union employees and requires employers to reinstate workers fired for union activities. The government lacked the capacity to enforce the law effectively, and the extent to which the government provided oversight was limited.

International NGO Freedom House reported in 2011 that labor unions existed only in urban areas and were largely inactive. The government recognized 12 unions at the national level. These unions, representing all economic sectors, were recognized after the 2008 elections and have a mandate that began in 2009 and extends until 2013. Employees in the private sector are free to join any of these 12 nationally recognized unions. Unions present in a private sector company form a union committee, which management is obligated to recognize. By law unionized employees contribute a fee of 2 percent of their basic salary on a monthly basis. Informally and not within an official union, artisanal miners organized themselves in small groups for mutual support and shared benefits. Workers organizations were independent of the government and political parties.

In small and medium-sized businesses, workers did not effectively exercise the right to strike. With an enormous unemployed labor pool, companies and shops could immediately replace any workers attempting to unionize, collectively bargain, or strike.

Collective bargaining was at times effective in practice. For example, the Association des Chauffeurs du Congo, which is the largest private transport syndicate in Kinshasa, declared a two-day strike on May 21, which was uniformly enforced across the city. Transporters were protesting the increased presence of police and national insurance company inspectors conducting roadside vehicle inspections since the beginning of May. In response to the strike and after negotiations, the government announced that it would implement measures to improve public transportation, including a temporary import duty exemption for new buses with more than 20 seats. The government also planned to purchase 200 buses to expand the public transportation system services throughout the country.

b. Prohibition of Forced or Compulsory Labor

The constitution prohibits all forms of forced or compulsory labor. Under the labor code, forced labor is punishable by a maximum of six months' imprisonment plus a fine. The law also provides for a penalty of 10 to 20 years' imprisonment for the enrollment or use of children under 18 years of age in the armed forces or the police.

Although no statistics were available, forced labor regularly occurred throughout the country. Violations included bonded labor, domestic servitude, and slavery. In the mining sector, individuals took on debt from intermediaries and dealers to acquire food, supplies, and mining tools and equipment. Miners who failed to provide sufficient ore to pay off this debt became debt slaves, forced to work to pay off arrears. The government did not attempt to regulate this practice. In the East some FARDC elements and many RMG continued to abduct and forcibly recruit men, women, and children to serve as laborers (including in mines in the Kivus), porters, domestics, combatants, and sex slaves (see section 1.g.).

Some police officers reportedly arrested individuals arbitrarily in order to extort money from them. The police forced those who could not pay to work until they had "earned" their freedom.

SSF forced men, women, and children, including IDPs and prisoners, to serve as porters, miners, and domestic laborers (see sections 1.c., 1.g., 6, and

7.c.). According to a 2011 report by Free the Slaves, an international NGO, elements of SSF and several RMG in conflict-affected areas in the East used children, including child soldiers, for forced labor in mines (see section 1.g.). Separately, the UN reported a decline in the use of children by SSF, noting a decrease in children separated from SSF and increased access to SSF encampments. At the same time, the UN and other international organizations reported a significant increase in 2012 in children being recruited and used by armed groups, most notably by the M23. The most recent reports available indicate that in 2011, 81 children separated from the FARDC (including ex-CNDP), while 141 escaped from various RMGs. The majority of these children were used as escorts, cooks, and/or porters.

The government did not effectively enforce laws prohibiting forced or compulsory labor and took no action against those who used forced labor and abducted civilians for forced labor. No official child labor investigations were reported. Little if any information existed on the removal of victims from forced labor. By year's end there was no effective government effort underway to limit child labor in mines.

Also see the Department of State's annual *Trafficking in Persons Report* at www.state.

c. Prohibition of Child Labor and Minimum Age for Employment

The child protection law of 2009 provides that the minimum age for full-time employment without parental consent is 18 years. Employers may legally hire minors between the ages of 15 and 18 with the consent of a parent or guardian. The law also stipulates that children cannot work for more than four hours per day and restricts all minors from transporting heavy items.

While criminal courts continued to hear child labor complaints, neither the courts nor other government agencies were able to effectively enforce these laws. Government ministries and the National Committee to Combat the Worst Forms of Child Labor lacked the resources and capacity to enforce child labor laws.

The Ministry of Labor has responsibility for investigating child labor abuses but had no dedicated child labor inspection service. Although the government approved a national action plan to combat the worst forms of child labor in 2011, it had yet to be implemented by the end of the year. Other government agencies responsible for combating child labor included the

Ministry of Gender, Family and Children, the Ministry of Justice and Human Rights, the Ministry of Social Affairs, and the National Committee to Combat the Worst Forms of Child Labor. These agencies had no budgets for inspections and conducted no child labor investigations.

The government did not undertake any measures to reinforce the capacities of the labor inspectors to ensure that children under 18 did not engage in hazardous work in mines.

Child labor, including forced child labor, was a problem throughout the country (see section 7.b.). Child labor was most common in the informal sector, particularly in mining and subsistence agriculture. For economic survival families often encouraged children to work. According to the Ministry of Labor, children worked in mines and stone quarries and as child soldiers, water sellers, domestic servants, and entertainers in bars and restaurants.

According to data collected by a 2010 UNICEF survey, approximately 42 percent of children between the ages of five and 14 were involved in child labor. The same survey indicated that children in rural areas are more likely to be involved in child labor than children in urban areas (46 percent compared with 34 percent). UNICEF considered children to be involved in labor if, during the week preceding the survey, a child five to 11 years old performed at least one hour of economic activity or at least 28 hours of domestic work, or a child 12 to 14 years old performed at least 14 hours of economic activity or at least 28 hours of domestic work.

Children were also exploited in the worst forms of child labor, many of them in agriculture, street vending, water selling, and domestic service. By some estimates tens of thousands of children worked in the mining sector, most often in extremely dangerous conditions as artisanal miners. Children made up as much as 30 percent of the work force in the artisanal mining sector. Children mined diamonds, gold, cobalt, coltan, wolframite, and cassiterite under hazardous conditions. In mining regions of the provinces of Katanga, Kasai Occidental, Orientale, North Kivu, and South Kivu, children sifted, cleaned, sorted, transported heavy loads, and dug for minerals underground. In many areas of the country, children five to 12 years old broke rocks to make gravel for a small wage.

Parents often used children for dangerous and difficult agricultural labor. Families unable to support their children occasionally sent them to live with relatives who effectively treated the children as domestic slaves, subjecting them to physical and sexual abuse.

Children were also trafficked for sexual exploitation, including for prostitution in brothels or by loosely organized networks. Reports indicated continued child prostitution, including forced prostitution, throughout the country (see section 6).

Also see the Department of Labor's *Findings on the Worst Forms of Child Labor* at www.dol.gov/ilab/programs/ocft/tda.htm.

d. Acceptable Conditions of Work

The government sets regional minimum wages for all workers in private enterprise, with the highest pay scales applied to the cities of Kinshasa and Lubumbashi. In January 2009 the government established a minimum wage of 1,680 Congolese francs (approximately $3 at that time) per day. Due to the continued devaluation of the currency, the minimum wage, which had not been adjusted, stood at $1.83 at year's end. In the public sector, the government sets wages by decree and permits unions to act only in an advisory capacity. By year's end the government had not yet set 2012 wages.

The law defines different standard workweeks, ranging from 45 to 72 hours, for various jobs and prescribes rest periods and premium pay for overtime. However, the law establishes no monitoring or enforcement mechanism, and employers in both the formal and informal sectors often did not respect these provisions. The law does not prohibit compulsory overtime.

The average monthly wage did not provide a decent standard of living for a worker and family. Government salaries remained low, ranging from 45,000 to 75,000 Congolese francs ($49 to $82) per month, and salary arrears were common in both the civil service and public enterprises (parastatals). The government began paying some civil servants' salaries in July through the banking system in main cities only.

The law specifies health and safety standards. Health and safety standards were not effectively enforced in the informal sector, and enforcement was uneven in the formal sector. Major international mining companies effectively observed health and safety standards. More than 90 percent of laborers worked in subsistence agriculture, informal commerce or mining, or other informal pursuits, where they were subjected to hazardous and/or exploitive working conditions. According to the World Bank, between 500,000 and two million miners worked in the informal sector nationwide and up to 16 percent of the population indirectly relied on artisanal mining. In August approximately 60 gold miners died in the collapse of an artisanal gold mine in

Orientale province. Overall estimates were notoriously challenging to verify, and determining the number of miners working in the conflict areas was difficult. In 2010 the international NGO Pact estimated that between 200,000 and 250,000 miners worked in North Kivu and South Kivu. Assaults by security guards and SSF on artisanal miners for illegally entering mining concessions were common.

In: Democratic Republic of Congo
Editor: Shelby Rake

ISBN: 978-1-63117-544-2
© 2014 Nova Science Publishers, Inc.

Chapter 3

DEMOCRATIC REPUBLIC OF THE CONGO 2012 INTERNATIONAL RELIGIOUS FREEDOM REPORT*

U.S. Department of State; Bureau of Democracy, Human Rights and Labor

EXECUTIVE SUMMARY

The constitution and other laws and policies protect religious freedom and, in practice, the government generally respected religious freedom. The trend in the government's respect for religious freedom did not change significantly during the year.

There were no reports of societal abuses or discrimination based on religious affiliation, belief, or practice.

U.S. embassy representatives discussed religious freedom with the government and routinely met with religious leaders of all faiths.

---

* This is an edited, reformatted and augmented version of a report released by the U.S. Department of State; Bureau of Democracy, Human Rights and Labor, dated May 2013.

SECTION I. RELIGIOUS DEMOGRAPHY

The population is 68.7 million, according to a 2011 UN Population Fund estimate. Approximately 50 percent is Roman Catholic, 35 percent Protestant (including evangelicals), 5 percent Kimbanguist (a Christian-inspired Congolese church), and 5 percent Muslim. Other religious groups with smaller populations include Jehovah's Witnesses, The Church of Jesus Christ of Latter-day Saints (Mormons), Greek Orthodox Christians, and Jews. The remainder generally adheres to indigenous religious beliefs. Approximately 70 percent of the population attends religious services weekly.

Most religious groups are scattered throughout the country and are widely represented in cities and large towns. Muslims mainly reside in the provinces of Maniema, Orientale, Kasai Occidental, Bandundu, and Kinshasa. Although present throughout the country, Kimbanguists are primarily concentrated in Kinshasa and Bas-Congo.

SECTION II. STATUS OF GOVERNMENT RESPECT FOR RELIGIOUS FREEDOM

Legal/Policy Framework

The constitution and other laws and policies protect religious freedom.

A statutory order on the Regulation of Nonprofit Associations and Public Utilities regulates the establishment and operation of religious groups. By law, the government may recognize, suspend recognition of, or dissolve religious groups. The government grants tax-exempt status to recognized religious groups. The law requires officially recognized religious groups to maintain nonprofit status and respect the general public order. It also permits religious groups to establish places of worship and train clergy.

Nonprofit organizations, including religious groups, must register with the government by submitting a copy of their bylaws and constitution. Upon submission, the justice ministry issues a provisional approval, and within six months, a permanent approval. At the end of this six month period and regardless of whether or not the ministry issued its permanent approval, the group is considered registered and approved by the government. The government also requires foreign religious groups to obtain this approval.

The government observes Christmas as a national holiday.

Government Practices

There were no reports of abuses of religious freedom.

Despite the registration requirement, unregistered domestic religious groups operated unhindered. Foreign religious groups generally operated without restriction after receiving approval from the government.

The government was primarily responsible for the administration of schools, but religious groups retained significant oversight and managerial independence. Approximately 72 percent of primary school students attended schools owned and managed by religious groups but funded in whole or in part by the government; 17 percent attended secular public schools, and 11 percent attended secular private schools. Of secondary schools, 64 percent were religious, 22 percent were secular public schools and 14 percent were secular private schools. Protestant groups managed 43 percent of primary and 34 percent of secondary schools. The Catholic Church managed 40 percent of primary and 21 percent of secondary schools. Religious classes typically were mandatory in religious schools.

SECTION III. STATUS OF SOCIETAL RESPECT FOR RELIGIOUS FREEDOM

There were no reports of societal abuses or discrimination based on religious affiliation, belief, or practice.

SECTION IV. U.S. GOVERNMENT POLICY

The U.S. ambassador and embassy representatives met regularly with the government and major religious leaders.

On August 13, the embassy co-hosted an iftar with Muslim groups. Over 100 people attended, including Muslims from the local and international communities, government officials, and non-Muslim diplomats.

In: Democratic Republic of Congo
Editor: Shelby Rake

ISBN: 978-1-63117-544-2
© 2014 Nova Science Publishers, Inc.

Chapter 4

2013 INVESTMENT CLIMATE STATEMENT: DEMOCRATIC REPUBLIC OF CONGO[*]

Bureau of Economic and Business Affairs

OPENNESS TO, AND RESTRICTIONS UPON, FOREIGN INVESTMENT

The Democratic Republic of Congo (DRC) remains a highly challenging environment in which to conduct business. At the same time, the current government has taken several steps to improve the business climate and improve economic governance. The DRC's rich endowment of natural resources, large population (approximately 71 million) and generally open trading system provide significant potential opportunities for U.S. investors. The DRC was ranked 181 out of 185 in the 2013 World Bank Doing Business Report, a slight decrease from the 2012 report. However, the DRC has taken concrete actions taken in 2012 to improve the business climate. Performance registered by the DRC in a number of indicators is summarized in the table below (Millennium Challenge Corporation (MCC) indicators are measured on a scale of 0% to 100%. The MCC indicators are percentile rankings of the DRC in its low income group):

---

[*] This is an edited, reformatted and augmented version of the Bureau of Economic and Business Affairs report, dated April 2013.

Measure	Year	Index/Ranking
TI Corruption Index	2012	160 out of 176 countries
Heritage Economic Freedom	2012	172 out of 179 countries
World Bank Doing Business	2013	181 out of 185 countries
MCC Government Effectiveness	FY 2013	-0.78
MCC Rule of Law	FY 2013	-0.69
MCC Control of Corruption	FY 2013	-0.50
MCC Fiscal Policy	FY 2013	0.2
MCC Trade Policy	FY 2013	63.0
MCC Regulatory Quality	FY 2013	-0.76
MCC Business Start Up	FY 2013	0.462
MCC Land Rights Access	FY 2013	0.48
MCC Natural Resource Mgmt	FY 2013	60.4
MCC Access to Credit	FY 2013	9
MCC Inflation	FY 2013	15.5

The DRC government (GDRC) has taken several steps this year to improve economic governance and the business climate. In January 2012, the DRC implemented a value-added tax that has increased government receipts without provoking an inflationary crisis. The tax, implemented at the recommendation of the International Monetary Fund, distributes the tax burden more evenly throughout the Congolese formal sector and encourages certain informal operators to formalize. In July 2012, the DRC took a step toward increasing consumer confidence in its national currency, the Congolese franc, by introducing new larger denomination banknotes without causing any inflationary pressure. In August 2012, the DRC also officially adhered to OHADA, the Organization for the Harmonization of Business Laws in Africa, which updates and modernizes Congolese business law. There will however be an adjustment period as the Congolese judiciary adapts to the new legal framework. Finally, in September 2012, the GDRC began paying civil servants by direct deposit, an important initial step in eliminating graft and patronage within the government. Tracking of government salary payments has also revealed fictitious employees and other mechanisms that perpetuated corruption within the government under the previous cash payment system. An improved customs code went into effect in February 2011.

While these are all important, positive steps, concerns remain over transparency in awarding and enforcement of contracts and concessions, particularly in the extractive industries. In addition, underdeveloped infrastructure, inadequate contract enforcement, limited access to credit, continued insecurity in the eastern part of the DRC, lack of adequate property rights protection, and high levels of both bureaucracy and corruption continue to constrain private sector development. The lack of reliable electricity poses a serious challenge to many businesses as well, particularly in the mining sector. Corruption and mismanagement have driven much activity into the informal sector, and there are significant legal and systemic restraints to adequate contract enforcement.

Congolese investment regulations, codified in the Investment Code, do not discriminate against foreign investors, except in some specific cases dealing with labor and related taxes. However, foreign investors, like local businesses, often face harassment and subjective, opportunistic interpretation of regulatory and taxation policies.

To overcome hurdles and to simplify and facilitate investment, the GDRC created in 2002 a one-stop agency called the National Agency for Investment Promotion (ANAPI). Independently run, ANAPI's budget comes from public funds and was estimated at just USD 500,000 in 2012. ANAPI uses Investment Code provisions to simplify the investment process, to make procedures more transparent, to assist new foreign investors, and to improve the image of the DRC as an investment target.

With support from international donors, the GDRC is also working to implement a series of reforms aimed at improving the business climate. Specifically, in August 2009, the GDRC launched the Steering Committee for the Improvement of Business and Investment Climate (CPCAI) under the Ministry of Plan with the goal of improving the GDRC's ranking on the World Bank's Doing Business report. The main objectives of CPCAI are to reduce red tape, decrease delays and the cost of establishing a business, improve transparency of procedures, and strengthen judicial security. CPCAI has reduced the amount of time required to publish the status of companies in the Official Journal to 48 hours and has also reduced the cost of obtaining a national identification number, two steps required to start business operations in the DRC. CPCAI has also achieved the elimination of 46 "zero-revenue" taxes among the 117 that were previously applied in cross-border trade.

In addition, the Steering Committee for the Reform of Public Enterprises (COPIREP), also funded by the World Bank but falling under the Ministry of Portfolio, seeks out foreign investors to enter into public-private partnerships (PPPs) to manage, reform, and revitalize ailing Congolese state-owned companies. Restructuring of approximately 60 Congolese parastatals, none of which are profitable, continues slowly. These parastatals include the national power utility (SNEL), port and river authority (SCTP), national airline (LAC) and rail company (SNCC). The government and state-owned Societe Nationale d'Electricite (SNEL) has begun to open the energy sector to private investment, and the Congolese Parliament will consider a law liberalizing the electricity sector in 2013.

Broadly, there are no formal limits or screening mechanisms imposed upon foreign ownership of most businesses in the DRC. However, the processes of granting permits and licenses in the mining and telecommunication sectors often suffer from arbitrariness, lack of transparency, and corruption. Investment projects which benefit from Investment Code incentives must have an assessment control completed by ANAPI agents every six months. Small businesses are subject to presidential decrees number 79-021 of August 2, 1979 and number 90-046 of August 8, 1990, which prohibit foreign investors from engaging in retail commerce. The government defines a small businesses as follows: a) Traditional companies that do not employ more than 10 employees, b) small transportation carriers that do not have more than 10 vehicles which do not weigh more than 7 tons, c) restaurants which have a maximum of 3 employees and do not have more than 20 seats, d) small hotels and e) small shops or kiosks.

All investors in the DRC face multiple audits by various government enforcement agencies seeking evidence of violations of tax laws or price controls. Foreigners and Congolese alike suffer the consequences of non-functional judicial institutions. Inadequate physical infrastructure – including internal land, river, and air transport, energy and social services infrastructure – presents a serious challenge and additional cost for nearly all commercial operators in the DRC. International donors and a 2009 multi-billion dollar Sino-Congolese agreement have begun to provide critically needed resources for infrastructure development, but significant constraints persist.

The DRC's macroeconomic situation has stabilized and the economy has recovered significantly from the war at the turn of the century and the 2009 global economic crisis. Mining activity in copper and cobalt is very strong, and there is ongoing industrial exploration of significant gold deposits. GDP growth for 2012 was 7.2% and is projected to be over 8% in 2013. The DRC reached the Heavily Indebted Poor Country (HIPC) completion point for debt relief in 2010, following a determination by the IMF and World Bank boards that the DRC had successfully implemented policy reforms under the program. As a result, the DRC received forgiveness of $12.3 billion in sovereign debt, freeing critically needed resources for poverty reduction programs. Several bilateral debt cancellations with the DRC occurred in 2011 for a total of $4.7 billion.

One trend of note in recent years is the propagation of so-called "vulture fund" legal actions against the DRC government for recuperation of decades-old unpaid private debts owed by DRC parastatal companies. These legal actions have sought to sequester and redirect profits and other payments owed by private multinational companies to DRC public enterprises through joint venture projects, including mining joint ventures. These "vulture fund" legal actions add uncertainty to the investment climate, especially for private multinational companies which are in joint ventures with DRC public enterprises.

CONVERSION AND TRANSFER POLICIES

The DRC adopted a free-floating exchange policy in 2001 as part of the implementation of broader economic reforms. The DRC has also lifted restrictions on business transactions nationwide. International transfers of funds take place freely when sent through a local commercial bank. The bank declaration requirement and payments for international transfers now take less than one week to complete, on average.

The Central Bank is responsible for regulating foreign exchange and trade. The only currency restriction imposed on travelers is a USD 10,000 limit on the amount an individual can carry when entering or leaving the DRC. The GDRC also requires that the Central Bank license exporters and importers. The DRC's parallel foreign exchange market is large and tolerated by the government, as the DRC's economy remains highly dollarized. The largest banknote in circulation is the 20,000 Congolese franc note (worth approximately USD 22), though it is very rare. Far more common are the 500 and 1000 franc notes worth approximately 50¢ and one dollar, respectively.

Exchange regulations forbid banks from providing loans that exceed 5% of their assets. Banks are permitted to provide investors with financing without a mortgage, if the investor has a good business relationship with his or her bank. The Central Bank is currently working on implementing a modernized payment system in the DRC that would allow businesses to use different kinds of payment tools.

Although the Congolese franc depreciated by 35% against the U.S. dollar between December 2008 and September 2009, it has stabilized as overall macroeconomic conditions have improved. The franc held its value against the dollar in both 2011 and 2012. The estimated annualized inflation rate in 2012 was under 10 percent, down from 18 percent in 2011. As of December 2012, the DRC held $1.7 billion in international reserves, sufficient for 11 weeks of imports.

EXPROPRIATION AND COMPENSATION

The DRC's land law allows for expropriation of property by the government for the sake of public interest, such as the protection of community heritage, completing public works (such as infrastructure projects) and the presence of precious minerals. The illegitimate acquisition of property is also grounds for expropriation. In any case of expropriation, the GDRC is required to offer fair compensation; as with many Congolese laws, these requirements are not always fully respected. Activities that have an impact on the environment, such as mining, energy and forestry are at greater risk for expropriation.

There have been no expropriation actions against U.S. citizens in the past year. Post is aware of a number of existing claims against the GDRC, some of which were taken to arbitration (see Dispute Settlement section below). Arbitration judgments against the GDRC, however, have not been paid in a timely manner, if at all. There are no laws forcing local ownership, although parastatal companies involved in the petroleum and mining sectors maintain minority shares of most foreign-owned projects.

In October 2010, the GDRC completed a lengthy review of 61 mining contracts dating from 1997-2002 between DRC public enterprises and private companies. The review, initiated in 2007, faced numerous delays and criticism over its lack of transparency. In 2011 and 2012, the IMF and the World Bank criticized several mining contracts that the GDRC concluded without prior adherence to transparency principles and called for the contracts to be published. The GDRC published all but one of these; as a result, the IMF's Extended Credit Facility program expired without the DRC completing the fourth, fifth, and sixth reviews of the program. According to a November 2011 British Parliamentarian's report, questionable sales of mines and oil assets owned by public enterprises have cost the DRC treasury more than $5.5 billion over the past four years.

A recent review of concessions in the forestry sector aimed at cleaning-up corruption resulted in the cancellation of a significant number of timber logging contracts. In January 2011, the GDRC announced the conclusion of the logging sector concession review process. The GDRC determined that 80 of the 156 logging contracts were eligible to be converted into new logging concession contracts. The GDRC required that the companies holding these 80 contracts submit a project management plan by the end of 2011 and address corporate social responsibility (CSR) issues. The GDRC cancelled the other 76 contracts, which it did not convert.

The GDRC continues to work with civil society, local communities and logging companies on implementation of post-conversion requirements. The forestry sector conversion process has been largely successful in addressing many concerns for the sector. Nevertheless, the forestry sector has encountered numerous problems, including the lack of enforcement of forestry laws and the marginalization of local communities by logging companies. Environmental advocacy groups claim that industrial logging operations are exploiting a loophole in Congolese law that permits "artisanal" logging of sites by local citizens to circumvent regulation of their operations.

DISPUTE SETTLEMENT

The U.S.-DRC Bilateral Investment Treaty (BIT) provides for International Center for Settlement of Investment Disputes (ICSID) reconciliation or binding arbitration in the case of investment disputes. In the case of a dispute between a U.S. investor and the GDRC, the investor is subject to the Congolese civil code and legal system. If parties cannot reach agreement, under the terms of the U.S.-DRC BIT, the dispute is taken to the ICSID or the Paris-based International Chamber of Commerce (ICC). A number of U.S. firms pursued claims against the GDRC for damages resulting from civil disturbances by military mutinies in 1991 and 1993. Two investors have won settlements from the ICSID. In early 2004, a claimant under the BIT won a settlement from ICSID but has not yet collected payment from the GDRC. The other investor, who successfully collected the compensation awarded by the ICSID, received damages in 1999. A third U.S. company won a settlement from a Jersey, Channel Islands court in October 2010, but has not yet collected payment from the GDRC.

The DRC is not a Party to the New York Convention of 1958 on the Recognition and Enforcement of Foreign Arbitral Awards. On paper, the DRC's official policies are satisfactory and even attractive to business, but in recent years they have often been inoperative in practice due to problems with the judicial system. Courts are marked by a high degree of corruption, public administration is not reliable, and both expatriates and nationals are subject to selective application of a complex legal code. Official channels often do not provide direct and transparent recourse in the event of property seizure, for which legal standing can rarely be determined. Seizures have been made via the police and/or military, often supported by questionable decisions from the courts. Foreign enterprises may have slightly better security of ownership due to the presence and intervention of their diplomatic missions. Many Congolese business contracts provide for external arbitration, but this is an expensive and time-consuming option with little value for resolving routine, day-to-day business problems.

In 2008, the DRC established commercial courts in Kinshasa and Lubumbashi for the first time, with additional commercial courts scheduled to be established shortly in the remaining DRC provinces. These courts are slated to be led by professional judges with expertise in commercial matters and may assist investors to address commercial claims within an otherwise inadequate judicial system. The DRC joined OHADA (Organization for the Harmonization of Business Laws) in August 2012. The core purpose of OHADA is to promote economic development and integration between its members, as well as to ensure a secure commercial environment in Africa. OHADA members agree to adopt a common set of commercial laws – including contract, company and bankruptcy laws – and to submit interpretation of those laws to the final jurisdiction of the OHADA court, which sits in Abidjan in the Ivory Coast.

PERFORMANCE REQUIREMENTS/INCENTIVES

The DRC does not have any barriers specifically targeting or restricting U.S. trade or investment. There are, nevertheless, some non-tariff related barriers present; including the multitude of taxes collected on imported goods by several government agencies and expensive, slow and burdensome commercial/customs procedures. The DRC has not maintained any measures that are inconsistent with the WTO's TRIMs requirements. The 2002 Investment Code is a simplified and improved version of its predecessor. Although there are no specific performance requirements for foreign investors, there are investment conditions that must be discussed and agreed upon with the DRC investment agency, ANAPI, to assure equitable treatment and procedures for all qualified foreign investments. The DRC has shortened this agreement procedure to approximately 30 days, and has created a number of incentives to attract foreign investment to the country. Pro-business incentives range from tax breaks to duty exemptions granted for three to five years, and are dependent upon the location and type of enterprise, the number of jobs created, the extent of training and promotion of local staff, and the export-producing potential of the operation. Investors who wish to take advantage of customs and tax incentives of the new 2002 Investment Code must apply to ANAPI, who will in turn submit their applications to the Ministries of Finance and Plan for approval. The Ministry of Labor controls expatriate residence and work permits. For U.S. companies, the BIT assures the right to hire staff of their choice to fill some management positions, but the companies agree to pay a special tax on expatriate salaries. There is no requirement that investors purchase from local sources or export a certain percentage of output.

Performance requirements agreed upon initially with ANAPI include a timeframe for the investment, the use of Congolese accounting procedures and periodic authorized GDRC audits, the protection of the environment, periodic progress reports to ANAPI, and the maintenance of international and local norms for the provision of goods and services. The investor must also agree that all imported equipment and capital will remain in place for at least five years. There is no discriminatory or excessively onerous visa, residence or work permit requirement designed to prevent or discourage foreigners from investing in the DRC, though corruption and bureaucracy can create delays in obtaining necessary permits. In 2008, the GDRC passed a resolution to abolish four burdensome requirements for establishing a company in the DRC, including the civil servant attestation, resident's certification, a document with the company seal on it, and a police background check certification. ANAPI and the Congolese Chamber of Commerce (FEC) play a vital role in addressing business issues in the DRC.

According to the terms of the Investment Code, the GDRC may require compliance with an investment agreement within 30 days of notification. Continued violations of an agreement may result in sanctions, including repayment of benefits received (such as tax exemptions) and eventual nullification of the agreement.

In the case of a dispute between a U.S. investor and a GDRC agency, the investor is subject to the Congolese civil code and legal system. If the parties cannot reach agreement, under the terms of the U.S.-DRC BIT the dispute is taken to the ICSID or to the Paris-based International Chamber of Commerce (ICC).

Foreign investors may bid on government contracts on the same terms as domestic investors. Foreign firms may even be favored in the bidding process because they can more easily access and present international insurance funding guarantees. There is no discrimination against U.S. or foreign firms in participating in government-sponsored or subsidized research and development programs, since participation is done on a national treatment basis. With the sponsorship and technical assistance of the World Bank, a tender board now works under the supervision of the Ministry of Budget. Normally, however, public companies and/or parastatals do not participate in the bidding process, due to the financing guarantees required beforehand. In addition, contracts are often negotiated directly with the GDRC, not through an international tender process, thus reducing transparency. Parliament passed a new procurement law in April 2010 and the GDRC has also adopted key implementing steps, institutions, and a manual of procedures to implement the new procurement law. The government said it would launch a public procurement website by December 2011, but it has not yet done so.

RIGHT TO PRIVATE OWNERSHIP AND ESTABLISHMENT

The DRC's Constitution (chapter 2, articles 34-40) protects private ownership without discrimination between foreign and domestic investors. It also protects investments against takeover, unless the investment conflicts with some overriding public interest. In this case, there are legal provisions for equitable and appropriate compensation for the parties involved.

Foreign investors can operate in the DRC either through establishing a branch or local subsidiary. The individual business may either be designated a "Société en Commodite Simple" (SNC), a "Société Privée à Responsabilité Limité (SPRL), a "Société par Actions à Responsabilité Limité (SARL), or a "Société Cooperative." The most common adopted forms of establishment are the SPRL and SARL, which are both limited liability companies. While in an SPRL shares are not freely negotiable, SARL shares are freely negotiable in principle, unless there are particular arrangements already within the SARL. Incorporation of an SARL requires a minimum of seven shareholders. Furthermore, incorporation of an SARL requires authorization of the Head of State. The Ministry of Justice is entitled to receive 1% of the original stock invested in the business by its founders. Some sectors, including mining, insurance, and banking, have different procedures for creating a company.

The GDRC has restricted one category of small businesses to Congolese nationals. This covers artisanal production sector activities, small retail commerce, small public transport firms, small restaurants, and hotels with fewer than ten beds. Despite GDRC restrictions, some foreign-owned small retailers, particularly Chinese-owned stores, have recently appeared on the market.

PROTECTION OF PROPERTY RIGHTS

Despite attempts to enforce existing legal provisions, protection of property rights remains weak and dependent upon a currently dysfunctional public administration and judicial system. Some senior-level officials are making efforts to restore and improve the legal and administrative frameworks, but the challenge remains to implement these changes at a practical level.

Ownership interest in movable properties (e.g., equipment, vehicles, etc.) is secured and registered through the Ministry of the Interior's Office of the Notary. Real estate property (e.g., buildings and land) is secured and registered at the Ministry of Land's Office of the Mortgage Registrar.

The GDRC continues to undertake efforts to improve legislation in regards to Intellectual Property Rights (IPR) and build capacity to improve implementation and enforcement. In principle, IPR are legally protected in the DRC, but enforcement of IPR regulations is virtually non-existent. The DRC's legal system and public administration do not have the capacity to enforce intellectual property regulations. The country is a signatory to a number of international agreements with organizations such as the World Intellectual Property Organization (WIPO), and the Paris Convention for the Protection of Intellectual Properties, which protects trademarks and patents. The DRC is also a member of the Berne Convention that protects copyrights, artistic works, and literary rights. The maximum protection that these conventions provide is 20 years for patents and 20 years, renewable, for trademarks, beginning from the date of registration. If it is not used within three years, a trademark can be cancelled. The DRC has not yet signed the WIPO Internet Treaties.

In July 2011, the Ministry of Culture and Art established the Sociéte des Droits d'Auteur et des Droits Voisins (SOCODA) to address IPR issues faced by authors. The Ministry of Culture in collaboration with SOCODA has presented a law to the government that seeks to rectify the flaws of the existing 1986 IPR law. The law is still pending Parliamentary approval.

TRANSPARENCY OF THE REGULATORY SYSTEM

Implementing a transparent regulatory system is still a challenge in the DRC. The GDRC is making some effort to improve the situation, including through appropriate legislation enacted by the parliament, but is still far from securing a complete legal and regulatory framework for the orderly conduct of business and the protection of investment. The GDRC authority on business standards, the Congolese Office of Control (OCC), oversees participation by foreign businesses.

There are no formal or informal provisions by any private or public structure, in any business-related environment, used to impede foreign investment. Problems encountered within the GDRC tend to be administrative and/or bureaucratic in nature since reforms and improved laws and regulations are often poorly or unevenly applied. Proposed laws and regulations are not published in draft format for public discussion and comments. Normally discussion only occurs within the governmental or administrative entity that drafts them and at the parliament prior to a vote. The Congolese public, as well as foreign and domestic investors do not receive an adequate opportunity to discuss or comment on these proposals.

In 2008, the DRC became a candidate country for the Extractive Industries Transparency Initiative (EITI), a multi-stakeholder effort to increase transparency in transactions between governments and companies in the extractive industries. The GDRC has taken some positive steps under EITI, including establishment of a National EITI Committee, publication of the first report on EITI in the DRC, and the hiring of an independent auditor to carry out the validation of the EITI process. However, the DRC did not meet its March 9, 2010 validation deadline. The EITI Secretariat granted the DRC a six-month extension (until September 9, 2010) to complete the validation. The independent auditor subsequently validated the report, and the National EITI Committee approved and transmitted it to the International EITI Secretariat in Berlin on September 8, 2010. The validation of the first EITI report was hailed as an important step towards improving transparency and accountability in DRC's management of natural resources. On December 14, 2010, the EITI Board designated the DRC as an EITI Candidate Country that is "close to compliant" and gave the DRC six months (until June 12, 2011) to complete the remaining steps in order to achieve "compliant" status. However, the DRC did not meet its requirements. The EITI Secretariat has given the DRC an 18-month extension until March 2013 by which it must become compliant or withdraw from EITI consideration.

EFFICIENT CAPITAL MARKETS AND PORTFOLIO INVESTMENT

Economic growth in the DRC since 2002 has increased the flow of money in the finished goods and raw materials market. Credit markets are also becoming more active, mainly in the commercial project and medium-term project sectors. All economic operators, foreign and domestic, have access to credit markets in the DRC without discrimination, as long as they can provide credible guarantees. Foreign investors, though, are more likely to benefit from this type of credit, since they are able to provide guarantees and collateral secured by foreign banks.

The Congolese Banking system has been significantly transformed and continues to improve, with new regulations and guidelines seeking to increase stability and promote expansion. While the banking sector appears to be booming, the banking penetration rate remains extremely low around two percent, which placed DRC among one of the most under banked nations in the world. With the exceptions of Kinshasa, Bas Congo and Katanga, the remaining DRC provinces do not have adequate banking coverage.

As of December 2012, there were 21 commercial banks and one development bank, SOFIDE (Societe Financiere de Development). All 21 banks are supported primarily with foreign capital. The DRC has additional regulated financial intermediaries, including 43 money transfer agencies and 19 credit cooperatives. Money transfer agencies are more concentrated in Kinshasa and Katanga provinces, while credit cooperatives are concentrated in North and South Kivu and Kinshasa Provinces. In 2011, the government established a National Microfinance Fund (FNM). DRC has approximately 1.6 million bank accounts in 2012, most of which are dollar-denominated. The volume of deposits increased from USD 835 million in 2008 to USD 2.34 billion in 2012. The overall balance sheets of the DRC banking system increased from USD 1.9 billion in 2009 to USD 3.47 billion while the lending volume exploded from USD 49 million in 2000 to USD 1.4 billion in 2012.

Through restructuring and recapitalization, the sector has improved over the past three years, aided by significant foreign investment. From 2009 to 2011, the percentage of non-performing loans dropped from 20 percent to six percent. Total bank capital nearly tripled between 2007 and 2011. DRC financial services are almost entirely focused on short term financing: 75.5 percent of credits disbursed are short-term, less than one year. The weakness of the legal system and the hostile business climate do not encourage banks to provide long term loans, despite the dire need for longer-term investment to finance the renovation and rehabilitation of the DRC's derelict industrial and agricultural sectors. Loans are generally denominated in foreign currencies, diminishing what little confidence economic operators have in the national currency. There are limited possibilities to finance major projects in francs, given the banks' limited holdings in the national currency (on average USD 12 million per bank), while foreign currency deposits account for on average 70.3 percent of their commitments.

Commercial banks generally provide loans to individuals in amounts not to exceed six months of their salary. Portfolio investment is not yet developed in the DRC. Business practices in the DRC are still at a fairly rudimentary level. Cross-shareholding and stable shareholding arrangements are not common in the DRC. There are occasional complaints about unfair competition between investors in profitable sectors such as mining and telecommunications.

COMPETITION FROM STATE-OWNED ENTERPRISES (SOEs)

The GDRC, with support from international donors, continues to work to reform state-owned enterprises (SOEs). To boost the efficiency of SOEs, many of which have been plagued by years of mismanagement, the government converted twenty of them from public to private companies in December 2010, though the GDRC remains the sole shareholder. SOEs that have been targeted for reform include those operating in the mining, energy, industry, transport, telecommunications and finance sectors. The government and state-owned Société Nationale d'Electricité (SNEL) have begun to open the energy sector to private investment. The next step in the privatization process for these 20 companies is for the GDRC to evaluate and determine their real value and their real debt. These companies' primary value exists in their real estate holdings, while they have serious problems with salary arrears, unpaid benefits, and huge unpaid debts to foreign creditors and to each other. Due to their inefficiency, these companies are not truly competitive in the truest sense, but they, their employee unions, and their other institutions occupy and congest a great deal of the economic space in their respective sectors.

CORPORATE SOCIAL RESPONSIBILITY (CSR)

Awareness about Corporate Social Responsibility (CSR) is growing, though largely among the large, multinational investors in the DRC, many of whom have formal CSR programs. The GDRC requires that mining, oil, and logging companies comply with CSR obligations before beginning operations. Under the Mining Code of 2002, mining companies are required to submit an environmental impact statement. Mining companies are also required to support infrastructure projects, such as roads, schools and hospitals. CSR provisions are also included in the 2002 Forestry Code, which requires forestry concessionaires to support social and physical infrastructure projects in the communities in which they operate. CSR is also reflected in the sustainable use of forestry resources. In November 2009, the Ministry of Environment, Conservation of Nature and Tourism held a workshop to analyze and propose procedures for local communities to share benefits from logging concessions. Participants at the workshop agreed on key principles that may guide the implementation of corporate social responsibility within the DRC forestry sector, including a social agreement that engages reciprocally both sides (the timber concession companies and the local communities) and payment by timber concession companies that would be made at two levels (construction of socioeconomic infrastructure on a per cubic meter of harvested timber basis and in-kind payment for actions of common interest). The local community would collaborate with concessionaires to fight against illegal logging and wildlife poaching and also participate in the sustainable management of forest resources. These principles were incorporated in a Ministerial Decree signed by the Minister of Environment, Conservation of Nature and Tourism in June 2010, which specifies the social responsibility requirements in a forestry concession contract. The Decree mandates the establishment of a fund to finance the construction of socioeconomic infrastructure with the payment of US $2 to $5 per cubic meter of harvested timber, depending on the tree species. The fund is to be managed by a local management committee composed of a representative of the concessionaire and at least five elected representatives of the local community and/or the indigenous people. Although the National Forestry Fund (FFN) exists as structured by the Ministry of Environment, it has encountered difficulty thus far in securing funding.

POLITICAL VIOLENCE

The DRC has suffered bouts of civil unrest and conflict for many years. Large-scale military looting in 1991 and 1993, for example, resulted in significant loss of economic productive capacity and flight of foreign investors. In addition, widespread looting and destruction associated with wars in the DRC from 1996-1997 and from 1998-2003 further damaged Congolese economic activity.

The country's first democratic elections in more than 40 years took place in 2006, under a new constitution that established national and provincial governments. National presidential and legislative elections took place on November 28, 2011. The National Independent Electoral Commission (CENI) declared and the Supreme Court certified the incumbent President Kabila as the winner of the presidential elections, although local and international observers reported that the elections were seriously flawed due to widespread irregularities, logistical problems, and a lack of transparency. Provincial and local elections, originally scheduled for 2012, are not expected to take place until no earlier than 2014, pending changes in the electoral laws and CENI's makeup in the aftermath of the 2011 elections.

The United Nations has its largest peacekeeping operation in the world in the DRC. Known by its French acronym of MONUSCO, it has over18, 000 peacekeepers deployed throughout the country, with a majority of them in the east. Violence nevertheless persists in the Eastern DRC due to the presence of several foreign armed groups and local militias, some of which have been loosely integrated into the Armed Forces. The DRC military has conducted a series of operations against the Democratic Forces for the Liberation of Rwanda (FDLR) and affiliated armed groups since January 2009. In April 2012, one of these formerly integrated groups calling themselves the M23 began an aggressive rebellion in North Kivu province, occupying large parts of the province and even occupying for two weeks in November the provincial capital of Goma. Supported externally from neighboring Rwanda, the group is currently in negotiations with the GDRC to end the conflict, although— barring full-scale security sector reform—a broader solution to the problem of armed groups is unlikely. Attacks, looting and exaction by numerous armed groups on local populations continue in North Kivu, South Kivu, and northern Katanga provinces, as well as the Ituri and Haut-Uele districts of Orientale province. Military efforts against the Lord's Resistance Army in Haut Uele has diminished its strength and operational capability, but small units of the group operate in and transit the northeastern DRC, terrorizing the local population.

In addition to continuing instability in the eastern DRC, chronic strikes by civil servants, public transport providers and teachers continue to pose a potential source of social upheaval. Military and police personnel remain poorly trained and underpaid.

CORRUPTION

U.S. businesses often complain about corruption in the DRC, citing it as a principal constraint to doing business in the country. The Mobutu regime created a culture of corruption in the DRC during more than 30 years of rule. This ingrained culture permeated the private, public, administrative, and business environments and has been difficult to root out. The DRC was ranked 160 out of 176 nations on Transparency International's 2011 Corruption Perception Index.

In principle, there are legal provisions to fight and sanction corruption. The DRC is not a signatory to the UN Anti-Corruption Convention. However, the DRC did pass its own anti-corruption law in 2004. Additional legislation includes the 2004 Money Laundering Act, under which the DRC cooperates with African and European crime-fighting organizations. Despite these reform efforts, however, bribery is still routine in public and private business transactions, especially in the areas of government procurement, dispute settlement, and taxation. The DRC is not a signatory of the OECD Convention on Combating Bribery. In September 2007, the DRC ratified the protocol agreement with SADC (Southern African Development Community) on Fighting Corruption. The GDRC is also preparing to ratify the African Union Convention on the Prevention and Fighting of Corruption.

The law calls for imprisonment and fines for both parties to a bribe no matter the circumstances. However, law enforcement remains a challenge in this area.

In October 2002, the DRC passed a law establishing an Observatory for the Code of Professional Ethics, which promotes ethical behavior among civil servants in the workplace. The Congolese Court of Accounts and the Congolese Anti-Corruption League NGO (in French, "La Ligue Congolaise de Lutte contre la Corruption") are also entities that work closely on corruption matters in the DRC. In order to enforce anti-corruption laws among civil servants and members of the government, in September 2009, President Kabila launched a "zero-tolerance" campaign. Within this framework, he established the DRC's financial intelligence unit CENAREF to combat money laundering and misappropriation of public funds. The DRC is also a founding nation of the International Anti-Corruption Academy (IACA) in Vienna, Austria, which aims to substantially contribute to the global fight against corruption by addressing shortcomings in knowledge and practice in the field. Its principal mission is to deliver anti-corruption education and training for professionals and practitioners from all sectors of society.

Corruption, including bribery, raises the costs and risks of doing business. Corruption has a corrosive impact on both market opportunities overseas for U.S. companies and the broader business climate. It also deters international investment, stifles economic growth and development, distorts prices, and undermines the rule of law.

It is important for U.S. companies, irrespective of their size, to assess the business climate in the relevant market in which they will be operating or investing, and to have an effective compliance program or measures to prevent and detect corruption, including foreign bribery. U.S. individuals and firms operating or investing in foreign markets should take the time to become familiar with the relevant anticorruption laws of both the foreign country and the United States in order to properly comply with them, and where appropriate, they should seek the advice of legal counsel.

The U.S. Government seeks to level the global playing field for U.S. businesses by encouraging other countries to take steps to criminalize their own companies' acts of corruption, including bribery of foreign public officials, by requiring them to uphold their obligations under relevant international conventions. A U. S. firm that believes a competitor is seeking to use bribery of a foreign public official to secure a contract should bring this to the attention of appropriate U.S. agencies, as noted below.

U.S. Foreign Corrupt Practices Act: In 1977, the United States enacted the Foreign Corrupt Practices Act (FCPA), which makes it unlawful for a U.S. person, and certain foreign issuers of securities, to make a corrupt payment to foreign public officials for the purpose of obtaining or retaining business for or with, or directing business to, any person. The FCPA also applies to foreign firms and persons who take any act in furtherance of such a corrupt payment while in the United States. For more detailed information on the FCPA, see the FCPA Lay-Person's Guide at: http://www.justice.gov/criminal/fraud/

Other Instruments: It is U.S. Government policy to promote good governance, including host country implementation and enforcement of anti-corruption laws and policies pursuant to their obligations under international agreements. Since enactment of the FCPA, the United States has been instrumental to the expansion of the international framework to fight corruption. Several significant components of this framework are the OECD Convention on Combating Bribery of Foreign Public Officials in International Business Transactions (OECD Anti-bribery Convention), the United Nations Convention against Corruption (UN Convention), the Inter-American Convention against Corruption (OAS Convention), the Council of Europe Criminal and Civil Law Conventions, and a growing list of U.S. free trade agreements. This country is party to [add instrument to which this country is party], but generally all countries prohibit the bribery and solicitation of their public officials.

OECD Anti-bribery Convention: The OECD Antibribery Convention entered into force in February 1999. As of March 2009, there are 38 parties to the Convention including the United States (see http://www.oecd.org/dataoecd/59/13/40272933.pdf). Major exporters China, India, and Russia are not parties, although the U.S. Government strongly endorses their eventual accession to the Convention. The Convention obligates the Parties to criminalize bribery of foreign public officials in the conduct of international business. The United States meets its international obligations under the OECD Antibribery Convention through the U.S. FCPA. The DRC is not a signatory to the OECD Convention.

UN Convention: The UN Anticorruption Convention entered into force on December 14, 2005, and there are 158 parties to it as of November 2011 (see http://www.unodc.org/unodc/en/treaties/CAC/signatories.html). The UN Convention is the first global comprehensive international anticorruption agreement. The UN Convention requires countries to establish criminal and other offences to cover a wide range of acts of corruption. The UN Convention goes beyond previous anticorruption instruments, covering a broad range of issues ranging from basic forms of corruption such as bribery and solicitation, embezzlement, trading in influence to the concealment and laundering of the proceeds of corruption. The Convention contains transnational business bribery provisions that are functionally similar to those in the OECD Antibribery Convention and contains provisions on private sector auditing and books and records requirements. Other provisions address matters such as prevention, international cooperation, and asset recovery. The DRC is not a signatory to the UN Anti-Corruption Convention.

OAS Convention: In 1996, the Member States of the Organization of American States (OAS) adopted the first international anticorruption legal instrument, the Inter-American Convention against Corruption (OAS Convention), which entered into force in March 1997. The OAS Convention, among other things, establishes a set of preventive measures against corruption provides for the criminalization of certain acts of corruption, including transnational bribery and illicit enrichment, and contains a series of provisions to strengthen the cooperation between its States Parties in areas such as mutual legal assistance and technical cooperation. As of December 2009, the OAS Convention has 34 parties (see http://www.oas.org/juridico/english/Sigs/b-58.html) The DRC is not a party to the OAS Convention.

Council of Europe Criminal Law and Civil Law Conventions: Many European countries are parties to either the Council of Europe (CoE) Criminal Law Convention on Corruption, the Civil Law Convention, or both. The Criminal Law Convention requires criminalization of a wide range of national and transnational conduct, including bribery, money-laundering, and account offenses. It also incorporates provisions on liability of legal persons and witness protection. The Civil Law Convention includes provisions on compensation for damage relating to corrupt acts, whistleblower protection, and validity of contracts, inter alia. The Group of States against Corruption (GRECO) was established in 1999 by the CoE to monitor compliance with these and related anti-corruption standards. Currently, GRECO comprises 49 member States (48 European countries and the United States). As of December 2011, the Criminal Law Convention has 43 parties and the Civil Law Convention has 34 (see www.coe.int/greco.) The DRC is not a party to the Council of Europe Conventions.

Free Trade Agreements: While it is U.S. Government policy to include anticorruption provisions in free trade agreements (FTAs) that it negotiates with its trading partners, the anticorruption provisions have evolved over time. The most recent FTAs negotiated now require trading partners to criminalize "active bribery" of public officials (offering bribes to any public official must be made a criminal offense, both domestically and trans-nationally) as well as domestic "passive bribery" (solicitation of a bribe by a domestic official). All U.S. FTAs may be found at the U.S. Trade Representative Website: http://www.ustr.gov/trade-agreements/free-trade-agreements. The DRC does not have a free trade agreement (FTA) in place with the United States.

Local Laws: U.S. firms should familiarize themselves with local anticorruption laws, and, where appropriate, seek legal counsel. While the U.S. Department of Commerce cannot provide legal advice on local laws, the Department's U.S. and Foreign Commercial Service can provide assistance with navigating the host country's legal system and obtaining a list of local legal counsel.

Assistance for U.S. Businesses: The U.S. Department of Commerce offers several services to aid U.S. businesses seeking to address business-related corruption issues. For example, the U.S. and Foreign Commercial Service can provide services that may assist U.S. companies in conducting their due diligence as part of the company's overarching compliance program when choosing business partners or agents overseas. The U.S. Foreign and Commercial Service can be reached directly through its offices in every major U.S. and foreign city, or through its Website at www.trade.gov/cs.

The Departments of Commerce and State provide worldwide support for qualified U.S. companies bidding on foreign government contracts through the Commerce Department's Advocacy Center and State's Office of Commercial and Business Affairs. Problems, including alleged corruption by foreign governments or competitors, encountered by U.S. companies in seeking such foreign business opportunities can be brought to the attention of appropriate U.S. government officials, including local embassy personnel and through the Department of Commerce Trade Compliance Center "Report A Trade Barrier" Website at tcc.export.gov/Report_a_Barrier/index.asp.

Guidance on the U.S. FCPA: The Department of Justice's (DOJ) FCPA Opinion Procedure enables U.S. firms and individuals to request a statement of the Justice Department's present enforcement intentions under the anti-bribery provisions of the FCPA regarding any proposed business conduct. The details of the opinion procedure are available on DOJ's Fraud Section Website at www.justice.gov/criminal/fraud/fcpa. Although the Department of Commerce has no enforcement role with respect to the FCPA, it supplies general guidance to U.S. exporters who have questions about the FCPA and about international developments concerning the FCPA. For further information, see the Office of the Chief Counsel for International Counsel, U.S. Department of Commerce, Website, at http://www.ogc.doc.gov/trans_anti_bribery.html. More general information on the FCPA is available at the Websites listed below.

Exporters and investors should be aware that generally all countries prohibit the bribery of their public officials, and prohibit their officials from soliciting bribes under domestic laws. Most countries are required to criminalize such bribery and other acts of corruption by virtue of being parties to various international conventions discussed above.

Anti-Corruption Resources

Some useful resources for individuals and companies regarding combating corruption in global markets include the following:

- Information about the U.S. Foreign Corrupt Practices Act (FCPA), including a "Lay-Person's Guide to the FCPA" is available at the U.S. Department of Justice's Website at: http://www.justice.gov/criminal/fraud/fcpa.

- Information about the OECD Antibribery Convention including links to national implementing legislation and country monitoring reports is available at: http://www.oecd.org/department/0,3355,en_2649_34859 _1_1_1_1_1,00.html. See also new Antibribery Recommendation and Good Practice Guidance Annex for companies: http://www.oecd.org/dataoecd/11/40/44176910.pdf.

- General information about anticorruption initiatives, such as the OECD Convention and the FCPA, including translations of the statute into several languages, is available at the Department of Commerce Office of the Chief Counsel for International Commerce Website: http://www.ogc.doc.gov/trans_anti_bribery.html.

- Transparency International (TI) publishes an annual Corruption Perceptions Index (CPI). The CPI measures the perceived level of public-sector corruption in 180 countries and territories around the world. The CPI is available at: http://www.transparency.org/policy_research/surveys_indices/cpi/2009. TI also publishes an annual *Global Corruption Report* which provides a systematic evaluation of the state of corruption around the world. It includes an in-depth analysis of a focal theme, a series of country reports that document major corruption related events and developments from all continents and an overview of the latest research findings on anti-corruption diagnostics and tools. See http://www.transparency.org/publications/gcr.

- The World Bank Institute publishes Worldwide Governance Indicators (WGI). These indicators assess six dimensions of governance in 213 countries, including Voice and Accountability, Political Stability and Absence of Violence, Government Effectiveness, Regulatory Quality, Rule of Law and Control of Corruption. See http://info.worldbank.org/governance/wgi/index.asp. The World Bank Business Environment and Enterprise Performance Surveys may also be of interest and are available at: http://data.worldbank.org/data-catalog/BEEPS.
- The World Economic Forum publishes the *Global Enabling Trade Report*, which presents the rankings of the Enabling Trade Index, and includes an assessment of the transparency of border administration (focused on bribe payments and corruption) and a separate segment on corruption and the regulatory environment. See http://www.weforum.org/s?s=global+enabling+trade+report.
- Additional country information related to corruption can be found in the U.S. State Department's annual *Human Rights Report* available at http://www.state.gov/g/drl/rls/hrrpt/.
- Global Integrity, a nonprofit organization, publishes its annual *Global Integrity Report*, which provides indicators for 106 countries with respect to governance and anti-corruption. The report highlights the strengths and weaknesses of national level anti-corruption systems. The report is available at: http://report.globalintegrity.org/.

BILATERAL INVESTMENT AGREEMENTS

The United States and the DRC (then-Zaire) signed a Bilateral Investment Treaty (BIT) in 1984 that entered into force in 1989. This treaty guarantees reciprocal rights and privileges to each country's investors. The BIT provides for binding third-party arbitration in the event of an investment expropriation dispute.

Germany, France, Belgium, Italy, South Korea, and China (PRC) have signed bilateral investment agreements with the DRC. South Africa and India will conclude a bilateral investment agreement with the DRC shortly. Lebanon, Ivory Coast, and Burkina Faso have negotiated, but not yet signed, bilateral investment treaties with the DRC.

OPIC AND OTHER INVESTMENT INSURANCE PROGRAMS

The U.S. Overseas Private Investment Corporation (OPIC), which provides political risk insurance and project financing to U.S. investors and non-governmental organizations, ceased operations in the DRC for a time following the events of 1991. Since the establishment of the transitional government in June 2003, OPIC has granted three political risk insurance contracts in 2004, another in 2005, and is currently reviewing additional applications by American-owned companies. In March 2006, the DRC signed an accord with OPIC that will expedite the process of obtaining political risk insurance and financing.

The DRC is a member of the World Bank's Multilateral Investment Guarantee Agency (MIGA), which offers insurance on new foreign investments to protect against foreign exchange losses, expropriation, and civil unrest. The GDRC is negotiating now for complete resumption of the MIGA program, which would allow for investment insurance in other sectors of the economy. The DRC is also a member of the African Trade Insurance Agency, which also provides political risk insurance.

In FY 2011, USAID launched new USG Development Credit Authority (DCA) loan guarantee agreements with two commercial banks operating in the DRC to help catalyze the availability of credit in the agricultural and small enterprise sectors. The DCA portfolio loan guarantee with one commercial bank in partnership with a large American mining company created a facility for leveraging up to $5 million to promote access to credit for small and micro enterprises (SMEs) throughout Katanga Province. In addition, USAID established a second DCA with a commercial bank operating in the DRC. This DCA will promote lending to micro, small and medium enterprises in the agriculture sector nationwide throughout the agricultural value chain.

LABOR

The DRC's large urban population provides a ready pool of available labor, including a significant number of high school and university graduates, a few of whom have studied at American universities. Employers cannot, however, take diplomas at face value. Skilled industrial labor is in short supply and must usually be trained by individual companies.

The GDRC sets regional minimum wages for all workers in private enterprise, with the highest pay scales applied in the cities of Kinshasa and Lubumbashi. Wages have not kept pace with the DRC's rate of inflation. While most foreign employers pay higher wages than the official minimum wage, the average Congolese worker has had to cope with falling real wages for over a decade.

The 2002 Labor Code modified the country's labor legislation, which is in compliance with the conventions and recommendations of the International Labor Organization. The code provides for tight control of labor practices and regulates recruitment, contracts, the employment of women and children, and general working conditions. Strict labor laws can make termination of employees difficult. The code also provides for equal pay for equal work without regard to origin, sex, or age. The code formally permits a woman to gain employment outside of her home without her husband's permission.

Employers must cover medical and accident expenses. Larger firms are required to have medical staff and facilities on site, with the obligations increasing with the number of employees. Mandated medical benefits are a major cost for most firms. Employers must provide family allowances based on the number of children, and paid holidays and annual vacations, based on the years of service. Employers must also provide daily transportation for their workers or pay an allowance in areas served by public transportation. Outside the major cities, large companies often assist by providing infrastructure, such as roads, schools and hospitals. Many labor regulations have been only sporadically enforced in recent years. The Ministry of Labor must grant permission for staff reductions. Generous pensions and severance packages are required by the labor code.

Every foreign employee must apply for a work permit from the National Committee of Employment of Foreigners within the Ministry of Labor. The right to strike is recognized and the law provides for reconciliation procedures in cases where the government is not involved.

FOREIGN TRADE ZONES/FREE PORTS

The DRC does not have any areas designated as free trade zones or have any free ports. The DRC is a member of the Southern African Development Community (SADC) and the Common Market of Eastern and Southern Africa (COMESA), but has not yet joined either the COMESA or SADC free trade areas (FTAs). The Ministry of Finance has already given funding to the

Eastern and Southern African Trade and Development Bank (PTA) to approve the DRC as the beneficiary of the bank. PTA would compensate for loss of DRC customs revenues when the DRC becomes an effective member of the COMESA FTA.

The DRC does have a "Special Economic Zones" project to encourage foreign investment, with a pilot project being developed in Maluku, under the leadership of the Ministry of Economy and Commerce and the Ministry of Industry and Small and Medium Enterprises. The government has not yet clearly set forth the particular advantages of investing in such a zone.

FOREIGN DIRECT INVESTMENT STATISTICS

Obtaining reliable statistical data on foreign direct investment (FDI) in the DRC remains a challenge. In order to alleviate this problem, the DRC Secretariat General of Trade, with assistance from the European Union, is undertaking a project to establish a Center for Research and Analysis of Commercial Statistics. There are currently two sources of information on FDI in the DRC: the Central Bank (BCC) and the National Agency for Investment Promotion (ANAPI).

BCC statistics are based on funds reported to the bank from actual investment projects underway, and are more accurate than those of ANAPI. These figures, however, may not capture all FDI flowing in the DRC; therefore, the quality of the BCC data is undetermined. Actual FDI amounts are probably higher than the BCC figures shown here. For the last four years, BCC has published the following totals:

ANAPI estimated that actual FDI in DRC as of December 31, 2012 stood at: $2.123 billion. According to ANAPI, the United States remains the largest investor in the DRC. In 2011, U.S. FDI stood at USD 519 million, representing 26% of total FDI for the year.

FDI (in USD million)			
Year	FDI in the DRC	DRC Investment Abroad	Net FDI
2007	1,808.00	14.30	1,793.70
2008	1,726.80	54.10	1,672.70
2009	663.80	34.80	629
2010	2,939.30	7.20	2,932.10
2011	1,686.9	90.9	1,596
2012	1,901.9	323.6	1,578.3

The following ANAPI-registered data are obtained from proposals by potential foreign investors. They summarize approved projects in services (including telecommunication, transportation, lodging, and electricity), industry (construction, mining, pharmaceuticals, brewery, manufacturing sector, and agribusiness), forestry / agriculture, and infrastructure.

FDI (in USD million)			
	2010	2011	2012
Services	512	1,230	1,635
Industry	757	697	470
Forestry / agriculture	323	39	18
Infrastructure	2023	61	
Total	3,615	2,027	2,123

WEB RESOURCES

- DRC Chamber of Commerce: www.fec.cd
- ANAPI: www.anapi.org
- Promo Congo: www.jcc.cd
- Five Pillars of the DRC: www.cinqchantiers-drc.com
- DRC Steering Committee for Investment Climate Improvement: http://cpcai.over-blog.com/

INDEX

F

J

L

M

S